"*Freedom* is a book for all of us who have struggled to deal with God's "no" answers to our prayers. Written with warmth, candor and wisdom, Nancy shares how God has taught her to live in victory over difficult circumstances that are unchanging. Her message is powerful ---- there is freedom for those who choose to surrender to God's plan, even when it is differs from our own and especially when it is painful. You will be blessed and challenged as you read this engaging book written by one of my heroes, Nancy Douglas."

ANNETTE BARTLE

WIFE OF MISSOURI SENATOR MATT BARTLE

"Jesus said we will have troubles. In *Freedom*, Nancy Douglas shares her story clearly and honestly, as a friend over a cup of coffee, baring her soul, and helping the reader to recognize God's faithful presence and peace in the midst of trouble. Reminding you "Who" to take the shards of your broken dreams, *Freedom* attests that--just like the Douglas family—God will navigate the troubled waters of re-emerging guilt, grief, and disappointments, to guide you to peace with the "new normal" of life. Regardless of the trials God has allowed for your life, you will be encouraged by reading *Freedom*."

PAM SHARITZ-TESCH

COMMUNICATIONS AND EVENT PLANNING PROFESSIONAL

Freedom

HEALING FOR PARENTS OF DISABLED CHILDREN

NANCY DOUGLAS

DEDICATION

This book and all I do is dedicated to my Lord and Savior Jesus Christ, whose immense love wisely grants me that which I *need* and not only what I want. Without you I am nothing.

CONTENTS

ACKNOWLEDGEMENTS

There are many people to thank regarding the writing of this book. Standing tall above them all is my husband Jimmy. As my only true love, he is also my greatest encourager, advisor, and comic relief. I had a vision of this book long ago, and you helped make it come true. Thank you for loving God, for never leaving me when the going got tough, and for being a wonderful father to our two beautiful children. You are my passion.

I want to also thank our son Drew for his willingness to be the first to read the material I write. I can't tell you what a privilege it is to work with you. You are so much more than a son; you are my dear friend and faithful co-worker. I love our time together, admire who you are, and thank God each day for granting our family with you.

For Cindy, my final editor: You have been a faithful steward with whom I trust my work. Thank you for all you do.

To my prayer warriors: Thank you for faithfully lifting me up in prayer. Only God knows all you've done to make this book a reality, and I will forever be grateful to you and the unselfish giving of your time on my behalf.

Finally, I want to thank our daughter Danielle, the catalyst of this book. You cannot read, write, or speak, but God has gifted you with a spirit sweeter than any I've ever known. I have immense respect for you and your ability to handle yourself against such odds. I can't express how much your father and I look forward to meeting you one day in heaven. With every limitation removed, we will discover all God created you to be, and oh what a wonderful day that will be! Until then, I give you all of my days dear child.

Freedom

CHAPTER ONE

The Storm

Something was wrong. I sensed it moments after her birth. She barely cried in the delivery room and hardly thereafter. As the tension grew I began to probe each maternity nurse with the same question, *"Is she alright?"* I feared each response, but had to ask.

To my surprise, each response assured me our little girl was fine. My concern, however, refused to subside. Something wasn't right; I could feel it in my gut.

Within 24 hours, my now standard question found its target as one nurse confessed, *"she's a floppy baby."* Surprised to hear anything other than the stock response that she was fine, I inquired into her meaning. *"She has poor muscle tone, which causes her arms and legs to fall to her side, unlike most infants who curl up in a ball when they cry"* she explained.

My suspicions were right. Something was wrong, even this nurse could see she was different.

Like the main character of a mystery novel, our little girl became more puzzling by the minute. She rarely cried, choked with every feeding, and was unnervingly distant, by avoiding all eye contact.

In a single moment our lives were altered forever. Cloaked as a happy event, her birth detoured our lives into a series of life-long challenges we could never have anticipated. Life, as we knew it, would never be the same again.

God had a plan, one that was grand and far-reaching, but not our own. With great precision our daughter was chosen to be His method to bring us closer to Him. It would not be easy, however, it would be the most difficult task we had ever faced in our marriage together.

It's been nineteen years since our daughter, Dani, was born Autistic, deaf, and Failure to Thrive. Back then it felt as though life as we knew it was over. It seemed as though happiness had suddenly vanished, leaving behind nothing but a vicious series of trials. Like a runaway train, we were heading to a place we didn't want to go, but there was no way to stop it. We were heading toward disaster and all we could do was hold on tight and pray for God to sustain us.

Our years of raising a disabled child have been difficult to say the least, but through it all, the hope of God was always there, shining through. Like a delicate tulip pushing up through spring's cold hard snow, God's faithful love brought its warm light into our otherwise dark, depressing, and scary situation.

Our journey with disabilities, has uncovered many curious things not only about ourselves, but also about God. The most surprising thing I've learned about God is how intimacy with Him is often established in the midst of tragedy. In fact it seems to be His trademark.

Countless times, just as I was about to throw in the towel, He was there encouraging me to not give up. Reminding me that His plan, one custom-built just for me, is about to unfurl. It is ready and waiting, but I must persevere and never give up. I must believe, trust, and follow Him.

Through it all, I've come to learn that desperate times, painful as they are, are actually precious moments designed to cultivate greater intimacy with God. It is during the hardest of times He calls to us the loudest, hoping we will hear, respond, and come to Him.

If you are reading this book there is a good chance you're the parent of a disabled child. If so, my heart goes out to you. The pain of disability is intense and almost sure to drastically change the course of your life. It takes you where you never planned to go and often keeps you there longer than you'd like to stay. It is a challenge of a lifetime, and a lifetime of challenges.

But, God is always at your side calling you closer to Him. He will never leave you and seeks to guide you through your situation. He wants to carry your burdens and take all your pain and heartache. He's been where you are and He understands what you are going through.

His first concern, however, is that you grow, not only that you will be comfortable. As we tend to focus on the here and now, He has His eye on our future and what we need to be strong, healthy, and firm in our walk with Him. With this in mind, our main objective should never be how to get out of the pain. Instead, it should be learning what He has to teach us through the situation He has strategically allowed into our lives. This new mindset makes all the difference in the world when seeking true freedom.

SUBMERGED INTO THE UNKNOWN

What is your greatest fear? Without a doubt, mine is definitely water. I love it in small amounts, and I know I can't live without it, but large volumes scare me to death. A shallow clean pool is fine, but I never want to go into dark murky water. There are too many mysterious creatures that love to graze your leg, none of which can ever be identified. Everything from its depth, contents, and cleanliness is at question, making me want to steer clear no matter the cost.

Then there are large bodies of water; they are the worst. The mere thought of being submerged in a huge body of water, like a pea in an endless pot of stew, makes me wince with fright. I am assured to know it was no mistake that I was born a 20th century Midwest Gentile. I'd have been a basket case trying to walk through the freshly parted Red Sea. Miracle or not, some dear soul would have had to carry me through, for I would have surely cupped my hands over my eyes and collapsed into a heap at the prospect of walking on land edged by walls of water on either side.

Beyond water, red or otherwise, anything unknown holds some degree of anxiety. It's a rare person who wants to go where no man has ever gone before. Feelings of uncertainty and hesitation are natural when met with the mysterious and unexplainable. More often than not we prefer to sit tight and enjoy a predictable calm. A little spice of life is fine, but only that which we can predict and control.

Unfortunately this isn't real life. Typically, the road of life is destined to dish out at least a few twists and turns that lead us to uncomfortable and unfamiliar territory.

Such is the road we walk as parents of special needs children. One moment things are fine, the next we find ourselves thrust into a world filled with great unknowns. *What is wrong with my child? What do I do next? How do I help my child? What lies ahead? How will we cope?* These are but a speck of the many questions we face once suddenly launched into this foreign and uncharted territory.

Entering into life with disabilities can be absolutely terrifying. Discovering your child is not as you had hoped brings a sinking feeling that can nearly drown your soul in grief. Great fear and trepidation can overtake you like a tidal wave, leaving you to wonder how you will ever cope in the future.

Moments of despair are unavoidable, waves of grief are inevitable, and feelings of resentment are nearly inescapable, but our ability to endure through these hard times hinges on one vital thing, that we keep our eyes on God and not ourselves.

Born the second of two children, Dani was our first little girl. Her brother Drew, three years older, was a healthy vibrant boy. He slept well, ate great, and played hard. All parents take pride in their children, but I was really proud of our son. I still am. He was exactly what I had always wanted in a child.

Like that special present on Christmas morning, his birth felt as though God had granted my fondest desire. Our experience with him made us anxious for another child, so we eagerly awaited the birth of our daughter.

My husband and I both wanted a girl. Long before she was ever conceived we prayed for her with great anticipation, then waited for the little one God would bring into our family. Without reason to believe otherwise, we trusted He would bless us equally the second time around, and He did, but not the way we expected.

God's plans stretched far beyond the blessing of another child. Far more than what we could ask or imagine, He sought to bless us deep within our hearts, in a way nothing else had ever done before. With our lives changed forever and futures heading for perpetual uncertainty, He had many great things awaiting us ahead, but first we had to be refined.

Once diagnosed with Autism and deafness, the little girl I had always dreamed of suddenly became everything I never wanted. Like an unexpected flood she came into my life, bringing with her the dark world of disabilities. I was confused, angry and discouraged and had no clue what to do with my emotions.

It seemed so unfair. Not only had I not asked for a child with disabilities, I quite frankly didn't want it. I couldn't imagine how God could ever consider her a gift, or why He would allow this into anyone's life. How could anything good come out of the situation? How could her and her disabilities be a gift from God? It was all far beyond what I could understand at the time.

My response to having a child with disabilities was a surprise to everyone, including myself. Friends and family naturally thought that I would be the one to readily accept our daughter's disabilities and assumed my husband would be the one to struggle most. I suppose, given my profession as a nurse, I would have assumed the same, but as it turned out nothing was further from the truth. When all was said and done, he accepted her and her disabilities with flying colors, while I failed miserably.

On the outside I grieved as you would expect, but inside, a wicked battle was underway. It was as if her disabilities had flipped a switch inside me, bringing light to a very dark side of me, a side I'd never seen before.

Caught totally off guard, and with no prior exposure to disabled children, I was thunderstruck. As if pinned against the wall, with nowhere to turn, I instinctively went to God. I asked Him questions like, *"Don't you care about this child? Why did you allow this tragedy? Wouldn't a healing be the best thing for both her and us? Where were you when she was conceived and where are you now?"*

Like dark clouds growing more ominous each day, these unanswered questions loomed over our heads, but more so over mine. With claps like thunder they screamed the reality of her disabilities in my ear sending jolts of fear throughout my body. Our once happy and comfortable life was now over. I was beginning to see what our lives were becoming, and I was fearing the future like never before.

THE FOG OF BITTERNESS

My fear of the future eventually began to take on a life of its own. Fed by grief and despair, it began to grow like a tiny unsuspecting weed in the corner of my heart. What began as normal legitimate feelings of grief, were now becoming major stumbling blocks in my road to recovery. My sadness of having a disabled child was turning into anger, exhibiting itself as bitterness and resentment.

Why couldn't my daughter be normal? I couldn't figure it out. I would do anything to bring her to the point of healing, but there was nothing I could do. No medication, no therapy, nothing. I couldn't adjust the past, I couldn't change the present, and I couldn't alter the future. It was all completely out of my control and it was eating me up inside.

Stuck at this impasse, I grieved not for weeks or months, but I grieved for years on end. Unable to move on, unhappiness became the norm. My zest for life had been dampened for so long that despair had become a way of life. Dani would never be normal and I would never be happy. That's just the way it was going to be. The fight to survive was hard enough, fighting for happy required more strength than I had to offer, so I gave in.

What was once foreign had now become familiar. Having been suddenly submerged into the life-changing world of disabilities, I was becoming accustomed to the pain. They say misery loves company; it became my close, personal, and faithful friend. I repeatedly cried, felt isolated everywhere I went, or took inordinate amounts of time wallowing in self-pity. These were now my customary habits.

It wasn't uncommon for me to periodically throw a party, a pity party to be exact. They were easy to throw. I could have one any time I wanted. All I had to do was reflect on what my life once was and what it had become. In no time at all a fiesta was underway!

I've had pity parties anywhere. Restaurants, church, department stores, parks, playgrounds, schools, you name it and I've partied there. I don't mean to brag, but I was a master pity party planner.

But there's a problem with having these moments of self-indulgence. They lead us nowhere. Like heaping sandbags atop our shoulders they weigh us down and grind us to a halt, hindering our chance of healing and greatly displeasing God, who wants us to be free. Determining to abandon this chosen behavior is vital and one we must all choose to do. Failing to do so will inevitably lead us down a path we will not be able to alter later down the line.

It is never God's plan for us to surrender to grief. Move past it yes, but camp there no. That is why He took the time out of His busy schedule of running the world to pay me a visit, a visit that would alter the course of my life once and for all.

It just so happened to be during one of my standard self-centered celebrations. I had only invited me, myself, and I, but He came uninvited nonetheless. What's a person to do?

The merriment commemorating my misfortune was fully underway when His presence began to shift the mood. No longer the main attraction, my attention was now on Him.

What could He want? Why was He showing up now of all times? After all those unanswered prayers from the past why did He come now, uninvited? I wasn't sure I wanted to see Him at this particular moment, but He was already there so I sat back to hear what He had to say.

With ears perked, I was ready for a Word. He began by first pulling out something for me to see. It was a diagram, a map to be exact. A bit odd for a party I thought, but it caught my attention nonetheless. This was going to be interesting.

To my utter surprise, it was a map of my life. As if standing before an upright Plexiglas map at the mall, He pointed to a particular spot. Leaning in for a closer look, low and behold I discovered myself on the map, and I was standing at a fork in the road.

My eyes began to stare deeper into the illustration wondering what it all could mean. Softly and tenderly He began to speak to my heart. He said, *"Nancy, you have grieved long enough. Today you are at a fork in the road, and the path you choose today will determine the rest of your life. You can choose the path of bitterness, and grow to be a bitter old woman, or choose the path of happiness, and determine to be happy in the midst of your trials. The path you choose today will be the path you will walk the rest of your life."*

My pathetic party ground to a halt as His words of truth began to sink into my heart. He was right and I believed every word He said. Deep down I knew it was true, and it was a relief to hear. I had gotten stuck and it was time to move on.

My decision that day was not a hard one to make. I missed being happy and He knew it. The thought of becoming a bitter old woman didn't sound good in the least. It didn't fit my personality. Oh how I longed for the day I could be happy again. How I wanted the weight of grief to be lifted from my frame so I could walk without pain and discomfort. His words that day revealed to me two things; I had a choice and He had a way. Like a breath of fresh air my hope was renewed.

Did you know we were made to laugh and have fun? Along with children, laughter and joy are a gift from God (Galatians 5:22) so we should always strive to be happy. God wants us to have fun and live life to the fullest. When we smile, joke, play, and have fun, it makes Him happy. Our joy is His delight; therefore we should never feel as though our lot in life is to be desperate, alone, or in despair. As children of God, it is His greatest desire for us to be free, content, and strong in Him. We should never settle for anything less that that.

It wasn't hard for me to make my choice of which way to go the day God showed me the map of my life. His visit brought great clarity to where I was and where I needed to go. I was heading for disaster if I didn't choose that day, then and there, to be happy. My decision to accept our daughter as His gift to me determined whether or not I would find true happiness. The disabilities were not going to go away, but He had a plan. Now I was curious as to what it was!

In one moment I changed the course of my life, and I am so glad I did. Bitterness had taken root in my heart and I hadn't a clue. I thought I was doing all the normal things a woman would do in my situation, and I was, but it was time to move on.

Once exposed for what it was, I wanted the bitterness gone. Like a broken rotten egg, suddenly I couldn't get rid of it quick enough. I wanted as far away from it as possible. My grief had become toxic and it was time to move on. I chose that day to be happy, and it was the best choice I have ever made for my family and myself.

It won't surprise you to hear that choosing to be happy has not spared us from further trials. We continue to experience our fair share, but God is always with us.

I continue to experience times of frustration when pushed to my limit, and the enemy is always there to tempt me to throw another pity party. But I always remember that day when God paid me a visit. I can still feel the couch give as the weight of His glory settled at my side and how honored I felt that He would take the time to show me the map of my life.

How merciful it was of God to warn me where I was heading. What a blessing it is to have been spared a life filled with bitterness and resentment. Seeing my true condition enabled me to change my course, so that I could begin to follow Him. Is He calling you to do the same?

What do you do when you don't get what you want? Have you taken the time to look at the map of your life? What road are you on and where is it leading you? Perhaps you are at your fork in the road and it's time to make a choice. Perhaps this is why God has you reading this book.

Maybe God is signaling a warning. Could it be you are on the road of bitterness? Might you be harboring deep seated anger? Are you stuck in a cycle of grief and cannot get out? If so, change your course now.

The longer you wait, the harder it will be to turn back. Given the warning I received, I believe there are points of no return in all our lives. Why risk going too far? Determine to be happy and choose to move on.

Paths of bitterness, resentment, anger, blame, and self-pity, only lead to a dead end, which is exactly where Satan wants you to go. He wants you frustrated, tired and without hope. In becoming so, we are rendered useless for God, and all joy, happiness, and freedom that is truly ours, is stolen.

Our key is to trust God! Only He can guide you onto roads paved with peace, contentment, and faith. He has a specific purpose and plan for you, which involves the very circumstance He has allowed into your life. In Him, nothing is impossible or beyond His reach. He can take any situation and use it for His good.

Is your heart hurting today? Maybe you've hurt for so long your heart is numb from the scars. Perhaps you've accepted that your life is what it is, but you aren't happy about it one bit. You cope but you have no hope. You're alive but feel as though you have no life. The storms of disability have shattered your heart, your life, your family, marriage and perhaps even your faith.

Dear one, take it from a veteran: left unchecked, these negative feelings will eventually drain every ounce of life out of even the cheeriest of hearts. You are no exception.

Wherever you are in life, it isn't too late to turn around. God is ready to show you where you are and show you where you need to go. All you need is an honest heart that is willing to change its course. Will you do that? Will you walk the journey ahead to find the Promised Land God has waiting for you?

Oh, how I pray that you will go where God is leading you. Don't be afraid to leave the familiar behind. God's plans will always exceed any of our own. They will never harm us or bring regret. They are perfect and just for you!

Look at the map He has set before you, listen to His voice, and follow Him. It is then you will begin to find the true freedom that awaits you.

CHAPTER TWO

Punctured Pride

The selection couldn't have been worse. There was only one style in two colors. I was disappointed to say the least, but we did what we had to do...we chose faded pink. Pale, dull, washed-out pink.

Dani was about eighteen months old when she got her first pair of eyeglasses. Already clearly disabled, the donning of these spectacles only served to worsen her appearance. She'd undergone surgery to straighten her eyes, but they still crossed and glasses only served to magnify this flaw.

I dreaded the thought of putting glasses on my little girl. She was mine, I didn't ask for them, and they didn't belong on her. In the grand scheme of things it was minor, but just the thing to put me over the edge.

Couldn't we just be done with it? At her tender young age, she had already seen two pediatricians, a surgical ophthalmologist, a developmental specialist, an ear, nose and throat doctor, and a physical therapist. She had been Failure to Thrive for no apparent reason, had two surgeries, was tongue-tied from birth, and suffered from chronic cradle cap, diarrhea, and diaper rash.

To top it all off, she exhibited the worst case of personality deficit I'd ever seen in my life. It felt as though all we ever did was give to this child, only to get nothing in return. No smiles, no hugs, no eye contact. No rewards for all her care. Just give, give, and give some more.

Life was tough and getting tougher; now she needed one more thing, something that would broadcast all her problems for the world to see.

We'd no sooner begun to adapt to her developmental issues and now we had to *"frame it"* with glasses. This was just great! Everyone and their dog would stare at us from here on out. Everywhere we'd go people were going to gawk and ask questions I didn't even want to think about. The simplest trip to the grocery store was going to be a big ordeal now that her disabilities shone like a morning star.

I admit I was vain about her appearance, but I wasn't too vain to give her what she needed. With the prescription on order, it wasn't long before her first pair of glasses arrived, and like a mule being led where she doesn't want to go, I went with Jimmy to pick up her first pair of glasses. I went like a good mother, but I didn't like it one single bit.

The glasses I'd seen in the past on other children were now on my little girl. Gone were the days of simply *feeling* different from other mothers and their children. Now our differences were visible. A neon sign plastered on our backs couldn't have advertised this flaw any better. The only thing that would have been worse was if I had had to wear these glasses myself. I wasn't sure I was ever going to get used to this new life with disabilities.

I was the first to walk out the door of the optical store, and I couldn't find my way to the car quickly enough. It wasn't enough for me that Dani could see clearly now, the only thing on my mind was the fact that she looked more disabled than ever before.

My body language screamed humiliation as I made a beeline toward the car, leaving my husband and daughter in tow. I wanted out of all that had become my life. I couldn't imagine what could possibly be next, and didn't want to know. As the stress continued to mount, I did the only thing I could think to do at the moment, dash to the car as quickly as possible.

I was half way to the car when something caught my attention. It was a sound, a rather odd one at that. Not fitting my mood or the occasion, it stopped me dead in my tracks.

Could it be what I thought it was? Surely not here and now after what just happened.

In disbelief I turned to confirm with my eyes what my ears were suspecting all along. Sure enough, it was exactly what I had thought; Jimmy and Dani were laughing their heads off.

I couldn't believe my eyes. Like two pirates inciting mutiny, they refused to walk in my wake. I was near tears and they were bursting into laughter. How inappropriate. What could possibly be so funny? Couldn't they see my misery? Didn't they care? It was obvious they were missing the seriousness of the situation.

As I gazed at the vivacious duo behind me, I noticed something else different about them. They weren't stomping across the blacktop in harmony with me. No, it was quite the opposite. Jimmy had placed Dani on his shoulders, and with extra bounce in each step, he was marching her across the parking lot. With each loping step prompting a thrilling jostle, they were like two clams on a wet sandy beach, happy as could be.

While peering at the happy twosome, their joy bewildered me. Not so much Dani's delight, but Jimmy's. How could two parents of the same child, respond so differently to their daughter receiving glasses? One had a loving focus on his child; the other on nothing other than her self. It was all I could do to keep from running away from it all, and Jimmy was skipping and laughing as if we were at a carnival. How could we possibly be so different?

Like a butterfly in the midst of a storm, his positive attitude amazed me. What was the key to his happiness? Did his affection for her supersede mine? Did I not love her as much as he did? What did he have that I didn't have? Why was I so miserable and how could a little pair of pale pink eyeglasses create in me such a violent stir?

Designed to bring her world into sharper focus, these little glasses did much more than help Dani's vision. Far beyond their original intent, they began to force me to see what was truly residing inside my own heart, something that had been there all along and needed to go.

WHEN PRIDE GOES BEFORE YOU

Why did my nose get out of joint the day my daughter got her first pair of glasses? Was it really the glasses, or was it something more? How could a relatively trivial event trigger such a hot-blooded response? Surely there was more to it than what meets the eye. Surely, it wasn't as simple as those little pink glasses.

Grief, sadness, and heartache are all very complex emotions. They are extremely powerful, and if not carefully monitored and evaluated, they can prompt us to do many strange and destructive things. With great skill they can incite us to do things we would never normally do, and lead to great heartache and regret.

There is a wonderful verse in the Bible that does a perfect job of unraveling my rather complex behavior the day Dani got her glasses. I wish I had known it back then. Perhaps if I had I would have responded a little better.

It's Proverbs 16:18 which says, *"Pride goes before destruction, a haughty spirit before a fall."* Though not a verse outwardly targeted to mothers with disabled children who need eye wear, it fit my situation to a tee. I hope it can help you too.

Let's begin by looking at two key words. First the word *pride*. It means pretty much what you think. It implies arrogance, pomp, and pleasure derived from one's own achievement. It's when we put our thumbs in our suspenders, puff out our chest, take in a deep breath, and hold our chin a bit higher and wait for others to see what we have done.

It is to be smug, haughty, full of ourselves, and quite simply put…a bit too big for our britches. Pride is the complete opposite of meekness and humility, and quite proud of it too!

Have you ever been afflicted with pride? Have you ever thought you were just an itsy bit better than you really were? If you're like me, you know it all too well. I've been guilty of sinful pride more times than I care to admit, and I suffered a severe case of it the day I stormed out to the car.

At a glance, the diagnosis of pride may not be what first comes to mind when reading this account of my struggle that fateful day. Maybe a broken heart, motherly concern, or grief would better justify such dramatic behavior. Perhaps pride sounds a bit too harsh and unforgiving; after all, I was her loving dedicated mother.

If the verdict of pride hits you a little wrong, you are not alone, it didn't sound good to me either at the time. I was in full-fledged denial, oblivious to it all.

But the truth always comes out in the end, and after years of self-evaluation, lots of prayer, and many painful experiences just like this very one, the time came when I couldn't deny it any longer. I was in a violent, bloody, fierce, and very real battle with my own sinful and dirty pride.

With each passing day, the reality of her disabilities began to sink deeper and deeper into my heart. Like alcohol on a beaten and wounded heart, each additional special need served to reignite an already throbbing ache deep inside, causing me to recoil in pain.

Each doctor's visit, newly discovered ailment, notification of further delay in development, and increased feeling of isolation were in fact huge antiseptics stored away for times such as this.

Periodic cleansings, which had to be done, often occurred when I least expected and revealed a side of me I had never seen before. It was never pretty and far from pleasant.

Out of the blue, suddenly I was exceptionally selfish, narrow-minded, and unbending. Wanting what I couldn't have, it felt as though a monster were living inside me and was about to burst out. Challenged like never before, this monster of pride was fighting like never before.

Now, I've fought battles with pride in the past, but never on such a massive scale. Losing a boyfriend, failing a test, and not making the cheerleading team hurt my pride, but not to this degree. This was a whole new ball game and the stakes were high. Dani's disabilities meant that I would have to sacrifice everything I had ever wanted in life, and I wasn't so sure I could handle it. I wasn't sure I wanted to either.

Truth be told, as awful as it sounds, I wanted out. I wanted out like I had never wanted out of anything before in my life. I wanted to bolt, run, escape, and flee. If only I could start a new life, then I would be happy. If only I weren't the mother of a disabled child, then things would be better and my life would be happy again.

I began to consider every avenue and alternative that could change the course of my life. I contemplated every option I could think of, but all were met with one minor hitch, my conscience wouldn't hear of it.

In order to escape my situation and start a new life, I would have to leave my husband and son. I would have to pack up and leave all that I loved in order to escape the pain, and the very thought of it broke my heart.

After all, they hadn't done anything wrong. Why would I leave all that I loved in order to escape this one thing? Leaving would only make matters worse. Besides, when I stopped to think about it, she hadn't done anything wrong either. It was just her disabilities I couldn't bear the thought of living with the rest of my life. I was stuck between a rock and a hard place. It didn't matter which way I turned.

In the end, the answer for me was clear. I had to stay. The pros of remaining versus the cons of leaving made staying a winner hands down. But the fact still remained. I was stuck in a place I didn't want to be, doing what I didn't want to do, and forced to give up my life for this one little girl. It was a noble call, but deep inside I was a coward brimming with destructive pride.

Which leads us to the second key word in Proverbs 16:18, *destruction*. This word means to fracture, break, afflict, or ruin. Interestingly enough, my Bible dictionary goes on to describe destruction in a particular way. It illustrates it as the "ruin of a dream."

Think about this for a moment and let it sink into your heart and mind. Apply it to your own situation and see what you come up with.

In a flash this one hit me between the eyes like brick falling from the sky. For the parent of a disabled child it shed a whole new light on the topic of pride, and it couldn't be more applicable to us as parents with children of special needs.

Let's take a deeper look together into what this means. But before we do, take a moment to think about your goals. What were your goals early on in life and what are they now? Have they changed over the years? Have any been met? Have some been altered? What former dream has been shattered and how does it make you feel?

I know exactly what it's like to have a dream ruined. My hopes and dreams of having a normal little girl have been completely shattered. In many respects it feels as though my life has been completely destroyed.

Future plans that were my hope for the days to come, are now but a vapor in the wind. Any independence I thought I would regain after my children were grown, is now gone. It will never be just my husband and me in our twilight years; it will always be three. All my dreams of rest and relaxation in my later years have been shattered, now replaced with the reality of caring for our daughter till my days are gone.

Instead of looking forward to the day I'll be able to do as I please, I am forever destined to a life of bathing, shaving, feeding, cleaning up, and caring for my daughter and myself. Any future independence in my golden years is now gone, replaced instead with the limitless boundaries of disability. My life has evolved into something I never dreamed it would become.

How about you? Do you feel as though your life has been destroyed to some degree? Have shattered dreams obliterated your life? Are you exactly where you *never* wanted to be, called to do precisely what you *never* wanted to do?

If so, you are not alone. These feeling are normal and come with the territory of being a parent with a disabled child. I dare say you would be odd if you didn't have these feelings. Life throws us terrible blows sometimes, many of which don't seem at all fair. We get what we never ask for, and then are left to pick up the pieces. It's easy to feel frustrated, angry, tired, confused, and alone.

The author of this proverb was acquainted with the devastation of a ruined dream as well. I don't know if he had a disabled child, but somewhere along the way he, too, experienced a significant loss that brought great grief into his life.

The interesting thing, however, is how he tied this devastation to his pride. Amidst the pain of a lost dream, he was able to detect the sting of pride. He didn't miss or deny what we so often find difficult to swallow. No smoke screen, disguise, or mask, he called it was it was, haughty arrogant pride.

When we replace this word *devastation* with this deeper Hebrew meaning, the author of this Proverb is warning us that pride comes before the ruin of a dream. The very thing he had hoped for and dreamed of had somewhere along the way become more his dream than God's. Becoming an object of his own pride and joy, he began to covet his dream above God Himself. Once the dream was ruined, the pain of loss brought great devastation into his life, because it was never rooted in God.

Where are all your hopes and dreams planted? Are they rooted in your heart, where they are fed and watered by your own selfish desires? Or, are they fixed on God's will and plan? Let me warn you that it can be very difficult to distinguish between the two. Like skilled craftsmen we learn early on how to label what we want as good and godly, when in fact it may have nothing to do with God's will at all.

More often than we may care to admit, once we sense that God's will is not the same as our own, we begin to rationalize, repackage, rewrap, and rename it, in an attempt to mingle them together as one. With our dream now packaged as God's will, we pridefully move forward in blatant disobedience, which inevitably leads us straight to destruction.

Please don't misunderstand. It is not wrong to grieve over the truth of your child's disability. It's also not wrong to pray for their healing and well-being. Only a good and loving parent does these things. What the psalmist is calling wrong, however, is allowing a ruined dream to destroy you, your family, or your walk with God.

What a tragedy it is to fall for the lie that says life has nothing to offer simply because we didn't get what we had hoped for.

How sad when we angrily pout for the rest of our lives because things didn't turn out as we had expected. When we do this pride gets the upper hand and we get the losing end of the stick, neither of which is God's will.

Having dreams is never wrong either. Though not all will necessarily come true, they serve a very valuable purpose. Like a breath of life, they give us something to look forward to, which in turn offers hope for the future.

Our ability to have goals and ambitions is what distinguishes us from all other animals. Monkeys don't hope for a greater tomorrow, they simply take each day as it comes. An extra banana is simply icing on the cake. Alligators couldn't care less if the creek rises or falls; they just swim and hunt as they were created to do, not caring one iota about what tomorrow will bring.

But humans are very different. We think, plan, imagine, calculate, arrange, hope, dream, and aspire! This is how God created us to be and it's a wonderful thing. What a blessing it is to look forward to getting married, having children, and raising a family. How exciting the anticipation is when we look forward to that new job or home. All these things bring a wonderful sense of accomplishment into our lives, and without them, we would be no different than the animals.

But, as God's prized creations, we are called to do something the animals are not required to do: we must put Him first. Yes, before all hopes and aspirations, He must come first. No matter how decent, moral, or attractive your dream might be, if it isn't the will of God, it should not be your dream. Failing to live by this principle gives an open invitation for pride to get a foothold in our lives, which sets us up for a painful and deadly fall.

Putting God's will above our own should always be our top priority, but it can be a very hard thing to do, especially when pain, disappointment, and loss are involved. It's difficult to accept that an all-powerful God, who could heal in an instant, would allow a child to be disabled. It seems so cold and uncaring for Him not to intervene, but in the end, whether we understand His method or not, we must place His will above our own.

It is during these times we don't understand God that the rubber meets the road. This is when our true character comes forth, showing what we are really made of. What will you do when you don't get what you want? How will you respond when there is nothing you can do to change your situation? What are you going to cling to when the going gets tough, a sad broken dream that will never come true or your faith in God, which supplies all your needs?

How you respond to these questions determines what you will do with your pride. Either you will keep it or you will lay it down. The choice is up to you and it is never an easy one to make. Accepting God's will over our own is a tough pill to swallow, and clinging to old dreams can be a very temping proposition. But whenever we hang on to our own plans and desires we end up forfeiting God's. As a result, the true freedom meant especially for us becomes yet another ruined dream in a long list of many that serves to devastate us even more.

WITH PRIDE COMES SHAME

It was my 43rd birthday. We were sitting in an elegant restaurant about to order our meal. Before I could decide what I wanted on the menu, my husband handed me a box, about the size of this book you're reading. As if pulled from thin air, there it was, a present hand-picked especially for me. Somehow it was already very special to me, and I hadn't even opened it yet.

What a pleasant surprise! In the setting of a beautiful restaurant with just my husband, son, and daughter, it was simply lovely. Jimmy looked so proud as he held out his gift, and looking across the table, I could see our son Drew beaming as well. Making the occasion even more special was seeing Jimmy teach by example, how our son should treat his wife in the future. It was a perfect moment in time.

"How did you get this in here without me seeing it?" I asked my husband. *"When I asked Drew to run back to the car just now to get my glasses, he brought it in"* was his reply.

"You guys are pretty slick," I said, smiling with box now in hand. "Should I open it now or wait till we order our food?" In unison both men gave the go ahead, so I gladly commenced with the proceedings.

To expedite the occasion, I forfeited the feminine temptation to gently pick at and peel off each piece of tape. Instead I dug into the gift like an African lion descending on its prey. The bow went to my left and the paper went to my right, all at record speed. Within moments I held in my hands a cream-colored soft velvet box.

What in the world could this be? I hadn't asked for a thing, but I talk all the time so who knows what I've said. My mind went blank as I tried to imagine what was inside this box, but two things were for sure; Jimmy never buys junk, and the look on his face assured me it was good.

With no further ado I began to lift the lid and peek inside. The dim light of the restaurant slowly began to enter the box, revealing its contents. To my utter surprise, positioned perfectly on a bed of pure white velvet, my eyes met with the sight of something I had refused to wear all of my adult life, a gold cross necklace.

Raised in a Christian home, I grew up believing in God and His Son Jesus. I loved Him and He loved me, there was no question about it. But somewhere in my middle years, my line of dedication to Him began to fog. Slowly but surely my feet began to gravitate toward the world as my beliefs became more and more masked by the ways of the world.

The line nearly vanished after high school, when I entered college and went wild. Doing all the things I should never have done, I now have a long list of regrets. Suffice it to say, I turned my back on God for many years. As a result, those were the darkest times of my life.

As horrible as it was to leave God, I always held a love for Him deep inside my heart. Too weak to show it outwardly by fully dedicating my life to Him, the only way I could manage to honor Him was in one tiny way, be it ever so small. I refused to be a fake.

Guided by an inner unconscious decision, I decided I would rather fall flat on my face in sin, alone without a cross around my neck, than drag His name through the mud with one on. Oddly enough, even in the midst of rebellion, that thin thread of love that neither He nor I would let go of, prevented me from further dishonoring Him by wearing a cross.

I loved God, but I was ashamed of Him, and we both knew it. I was unfaithful to Him in nearly all I said and did, and broke His heart more times than I'll ever be able to recall, but His faithful love was never far from me as He waited for my return.

Like a prodigal daughter, I went out into the world only to return when the pain of life became unbearable. Unable to fix life's problems on my own, I decided to run back to my first love: the God I knew as a child, my Abba Father and His Son Jesus.

Having been away for so long, I now knew what I was missing and I never wanted to leave His side again. With a new line of dedication now permanently etched into my heart, I was ready to do what I never could before, authentically wear a cross.

With tears in my eyes I gladly accepted my gift. The soft velvet pillow, like God's love, had been holding it for me all these many years, and it was time to pick it up and wear it genuinely. No more shame, no more rebellion, just obedience from here on out. I was 40 years old, time was wasting, and I had no time to lose. Things were going to be different from here on out.

Pride leads us to do many strange things. One minute we exalt ourselves high above God Himself, the next we're face down in the dirt, full of shame and disgrace. Both are common, unhealthy, and not from God.

I felt shame when Dani got her first pair of glasses, and was equally ashamed of God the better part of my adult life. I love them both deeply, but something always managed to override my ability to completely put them first.

Proverbs 11:2 does well to describe the demeaning power pride can have in our lives when it says,

"When pride comes, then comes disgrace,

but with humility comes wisdom." (NIV)

The word *disgrace* in the King James Version is *shame*. This means dishonor, reproach, and confusion. In a nutshell it says that our sinful pride brings disgrace and confusion into our lives.

When you stop and think about it, this makes perfect sense. James tells us that the cause of all fights and quarrels comes from within ourselves. We want what we cannot have, so we fight. We ask God for something but do not receive it because our motives are wrong (James 4:1-3). In the end all that remains is shame and confusion.

Have you ever been ashamed of God? Perhaps you wanted something so badly you looked like a fool trying to get it. When was the last time pride got a hold of you and literally took control? We are all capable of falling because of our pride. Our goal is to detect this pride and rid ourselves of it as soon as we possibly can.

James's description of the human condition reminds me of the cabbage patch doll craze back in the 80's. During the Christmas shopping season, mothers fought tooth and nail to get a particular doll. They hit, scratched, snatched, and trampled to get what they wanted, all for a toy.

Many women got the doll they wanted, but they looked outrageous in the process. Throwing holiday spirit out the window, they allowed their unadulterated greed to spread like wild fire. In the end, all that remained were shame and confusion.

Don't ever believe the Bible is obsolete or outdated. James witnessed similar behavior back in his day, only he didn't have to watch it on the evening news. Being the half brother of Jesus he watched firsthand the battle between man's pride and God's will. Culminating in history's most chaotic and violent event, man's sinful pride crucified his innocent brother and Lord.

What battle is going on inside you today? Do you feel confused by how you feel inside, or perhaps even guilty? Maybe you feel trapped and want to run as I did in the optical store parking lot. If so, I can guarantee pride is at the root of it all.

You don't have to be a crazed cabbage patch mother to exhibit the shameful disgrace of pride. We all battle it on a daily basis; unfortunately, only a few fight back. This is why we must continually evaluate why we do what we do, and why we feel the way we feel. If you are feeling trapped, discontent, and uneasy, the enemy is hard at work on you and there is a good chance your pride is at war with the will of God.

Is it time for you to let go of your old dreams? It is hard to do at first, but rest assured, God has a greater dream for you. He is waiting to bless you in a mighty way, but He cannot do it unless you first let go of the past. Give Him your broken hopes and dreams and then watch what He can do with them. You will be utterly amazed!

CHAPTER THREE

Good Grief

Her name is Hannah, and her story reads like a docudrama. Though deeply loved by her husband, any joy she once had was quickly snuffed out by the hatred of another woman. Jealous for her husband's greater affection, this other woman made a special point to ensure Hannah's life was a living hell.

Like a corrosive drip of water, her taunts pushed Hannah to the point of tears and anorexia. As one holding the upper hand, her opponent refused to cease her painful assaults, making misery an everyday norm.

Year after year, Hannah endured the searing pain of countless darts thrown at exceptionally close range. With the hint of polite charades long since gone, each dart was thrown with greater precision. Making matters worse, avoiding these attacks was nearly impossible since both victim and foe lived under the same roof.

Like a wound reopened with each sunrise, Hannah's heartache was nearly more than she could bear. Not a day would go by that she was not reminded of the pain deep inside her heart, and like blood, the scent of her distress became a delicacy her adversary craved insatiably.

Barren for no apparent reason, Hannah's infertility haunted her like a phantom every moment of every day. Whether alone or in a crowd, this curse had become her identity. She was the childless woman, an outcast forgotten by God.

Hannah is no longer alive. She died thousands of years ago, along with her cruel adversary. Her story, however, not only grips the heart of all who read it, but is one we all can learn from, barren or otherwise.

Blessed for her faithfulness to God, Hannah's life ended far from where it began. From the bleak existence of infertility, this woman of faith eventually became the bustling mother of six! With infertility a distant memory of the past, she busily cared for four sons and two daughters. Diapering, feeding, cleaning up after, and tending to a half a dozen prized children (1 Samuel 2:21) she was blessed beyond measure with a quiver full of children.

Her story doesn't end, however, with a full house. The challenge to remain faithful to God in the midst of pain and loss continued to be one of the biggest obstacles she faced the rest of her life. The good news is she passed with flying colors, and this, dear friend, is where we will find our true and lasting hope.

THE COMMON DENOMINATOR

Hannah's pain of infertility strikes a familiar cord in my heart. Though never barren, my husband and I know all too well the sting that heartache can bring. I used to think our pain was unique because we had a disabled child, but I no longer believe this to be true. Every single one of us experiences loss at one time or another. It is a common denominator woven into all of our lives. I wish I had understood grief better in our earlier years with Dani. Perhaps I would have been able to move forward sooner than I actually did.

The problem started back in my earlier years, I believed a myth that couldn't have been further from the truth. It's a myth many others believe as well, especially parents of disabled children. It's the myth that says grief *only* comes through a loss that results from death.

As a child, my theory was supported by what I watched on television; therefore, it had to be true. Over and over women in the westerns were happy when their men lived and sad when they died. Not a tear would have been shed if Old Yeller had lived, but our hearts were torn to pieces because he died. And Charlotte's web, now there's a page-wetting classic. It always broke my heart to think about how this endearing spider died before she could see her thousands of eight-legged children.

Why do these classics tug at our heartstrings and feel so real? What makes us cry every time we see them, no matter how many times it's been? It's because they are connected with one common thread, the grief over the death of a loved one. Hence my misguided theory on grief.

From experience I can tell you that living by this motto is devastating. As if learning to cope with my shattered dreams wasn't enough, I was in the midst of tremendous grief and didn't have a clue. Miserable for years long after Dani's birth, I never understood why. She hadn't died so the prospect that I could be grieving was out of the picture.

In tidy fashion I had compartmentalized grief with death together as one. Any other scenario never entered my mind. In the end, I was left with no explanation for the devastation I felt. I had no clue why I felt so damaged and destroyed, leaving the burden of unexplained heartache in my lap once again. No answer, no healing, no freedom.

My belief that grief only comes when a loved one dies was a lie. Grief can result of any loss, no matter the form. Whether it's the loss of a dream, loss of health, failed endeavor, lost youth, wayward child, you name it, if you lost something, you may well experience grief.

The birth of a special needs child is no exception and in fact can trigger a greater degree of grief. As a life-long call to surrender your life for another, the ramifications of suddenly finding yourself parenting a child with a disability can be overwhelming. Stealing our right to grieve only magnifies the pain.

As parents of disabled children we have every right to grieve and in fact we should. Failing to do so will only hinder our ability to move forward. It is important to see grief for what it is, understand the effects it can have on our lives, and seek to move beyond its bounds in order to fulfill the plan God has for our child, our families, and us.

GRIEF: IT CHANGES US

Whether you choose to recognize your grief or not, one thing is for sure, you will be changed. Accepting it exists or not is irrelevant. No matter what you do you will never be able to escape its transforming power. The question is *how* will you be altered.

Hannah and Peninnah are perfect examples of what pain can do to a person. We met both women earlier, but only one by name. Hannah was the mother of Samuel, who suffered infertility for many years, and Peninnah, her husband's other wife, suffered the sting of not having her husband's full affection. Each having what the other one wanted, both lived a miserable existence as grief took its toll on them.

Pushed to her breaking point, the true character of each woman eventually came shining through. Other than being married to the same man, they couldn't have been more different. Hannah and Peninnah clashed in nearly every way possible. How they responded to grief was no exception.

Day after day envy, resentment, anger, and pain worked hard on each woman. Like an accelerant, hostility and bitterness were ignited in Peninnah, while Hannah allowed the pain to bring her closer to the heart of God. Polar opposites in every way, each woman ended up as far away from one another as the East is from the West.

What made Hannah seek God in the midst of her pain, while Peninnah's heart was eaten up with animosity? How could two women respond so differently to the same emotion?

The Bible never mentions Hannah ever repaying Peninnah for the years of pain she inflicted on her. Clearly it was her enemy's goal to make her life a living hell, but Hannah never once retaliated. It simply wasn't a part of who she was. She was a godly woman who loved her Lord, and not even this painful thorn, planted so deeply in her side, could pull her away from Him.

What I find most admirable about Hannah is the fact she endured such pain from so many different sources. Afflicted with infertility, persecution, being misunderstood, and ultimately having to give up her firstborn son, she never allowed her grief to affect her negatively. By faith she took all her pain to God and laid it at His feet. Her trust in God is utterly amazing.

I love the account of Hannah's life because she is the perfect example of how we should respond in our own trials. No doubt that's why her story is in the Bible. So we can learn and grow from her experiences in a positive way, and not become like her nemesis. Hannah's life is proof positive that hardships will alter us, but it doesn't have to be for the bad. They can indeed change us for the good, and the choice is entirely up to us.

GRIEF: IT'S OFTEN MISUNDERSTOOD

I am humbled by Hannah and the life she chose to lead. Just when I think I have problems, I think of her and want to bite my tongue. How could I ever complain about my life, after all she went through? Would I rather live her life than mine? Not in a million years.

Though I could itemize a long list of piddly problems, none of them can hold a candle to what Hannah had to endure. The heartaches in her life must have felt like a torrential downpour at times. For years on end nothing went right for her, and it must have seemed as if God had turned a deaf ear to her prayers. Then, as if her existing pain and persecution hadn't been enough, she had to endure the exasperating feeling of being misunderstood.

Like salt to her already aching wounds, no one around her understood what she was going through. Making matters worse, the two men who should have seen the signs, were the ones who misinterpreted her the most.

Who were these callous men anyway? I wish we could say they didn't know her and were strangers who got the wrong impression in passing. But they weren't. They were two very important and trustworthy men in her life who were in fact very close to her. One was her beloved husband; the other her priest, a man of God.

Have you ever felt the frustration of being misunderstood? It's a terrible feeling. Nothing's worse than saying one thing then hearing it come back as something entirely different. I find it highly aggravating when it happens in insignificant matters, but to be misunderstood in the midst of great grief is beyond exasperating.

The two men in Hannah's life, and their inability to recognize her grief, illustrate the two ways our grief can be misunderstood: 1) Failure to understand what we need to ease our pain. 2) Misinterpreting our response to grief.

For instance Hannah's husband, Elkanah, loved her deeply. Blinded by his own love for her he figured it had to be enough to satisfy her every need (1Samuel 1:8). Yes, she was barren, but his love was abundant, certainly more than enough to fill her void. At least that was his perspective on the issue at the time.

As egotistical as this may sound, I believe Elkanah meant well. He did not fully understand what she was going through, but his heart was in the right place. He offered her the most precious gift he had, his undying love, and trusted it to be enough to ease her pain.

I defend Elkanah because scripture clearly acknowledged his love for her. It was quite evident and unparalleled, so much so, it was the very thing that triggered Peninnah's wicked behavior. Were it not for his greater love, much of Hannah's grief would have indeed been spared.

But as real, strong, and unmistakable as Elkanah's love for Hannah was, it wasn't enough to erase the grief of her barren womb. That was something only she could do, on her own, alone with God.

Then there was Eli, her priest, who misunderstood her altogether. Scripture paints a most vivid picture of his warped analysis: *"As she kept on praying to the LORD, Eli observed her mouth. Hannah was praying in her heart, and her lips were moving but her voice was not heard. Eli thought she was drunk and said to her, "How long will you keep on getting drunk? Get rid of your wine"* (1 Samuel 1:12-14).

Everywhere she turned, no one understood her grief. Not the man she loved, or the man of God. It must have felt like the Twightlight Zone. At home, in the house of God, at the market, in the streets, no one understood the pain she was going through. Isolated, alone, and distraught, Hannah was grossly misunderstood by everyone around her, and there wasn't a thing she could do about it.

Wrong impressions, insensitive remarks, and casual quick fixes, can devastate the heart. I don't think we can ever be fully prepared for the impact they can have on our hearts. Once said, these hollow words of wisdom, if not carefully buffered, can sink deep into our hearts and begin to take root. Before we know it, frustration, anger, and disappointment become a part of who we are.

During some of my most intense times of grieving, I had many well-meaning individuals cave in to the urge of attempting to relieve my pain, only to inflict more in the process.

I can't count the times I've been told how fortunate we are to have Dani, and how special we are to be chosen as her parents. While these comments may well be true, they don't address the real issue. These people meant well, but didn't have a clue what I was really going through. Good intentions weren't enough. In the end they only left me feeling alone and misunderstood again.

Of all the pearls of wisdom that have been tossed my way, only one gem was worth keeping, and it made an unforgettably positive impact on me. It was a comment from a fellow nurse in the wee hours of the morning during a nightshift. After updating her on Dani's condition, she simply replied, *"Nancy, I have absolutely no idea what you must be going through."*

That's it. That was all she said, yet it brought me the greatest sense of relief and peace. Finally, for once someone wasn't telling me how to feel or attempting to give a pithy solution to my complex problems. She didn't have a clue what my life was like and she acknowledged it. I treasured her honesty and thanked her for those soothing words of comfort.

I still savor that moment and the words she said to me in the middle of the night. It's a rare occasion that someone acknowledges my grief then lets me be who I am in the midst of the pain. No judgments, no timelines, no opinions, no solutions, and no critiques, just the simple recognition of my pain and the approval to feel it. Oh I know I am going to feel the heartache whether they consent to it or not, it just helps when someone comes alongside and puts her arm around you in the process.

TRIGGERS OF GRIEF

There's nothing like having a good day, and then suddenly the bottom drops out. In a flash, you feel as though you've been hit in the head with a brick. Suddenly you find yourself dazed and confused trying to figure out what went wrong.

Perhaps it was the site of someone else's healthy child, one who looked similar to the one you once dreamed of having. Or maybe it was a comment that hit you the wrong way, or another unexplainable wave of depression. Whatever it was, one minute you were fine, the next you were flat on your face and you didn't know why.

Living through grief is like walking a minefield. You never know when a bomb is going to detonate and rattle your world. Unable to predict when it will hit or how you will fare, simple daily routines can become unsettling.

These are the triggers of grief. Planted all around us, they wait till we come near, and then when we least expect it, explode with forces that can derail us for days, weeks, or months. Just one sight, word, or thought is enough to tip us over the edge and steal our joy.

Though triggers of grief are far too numerous to count, we can begin to look for them by knowing the three main categories they fall into. Once you know these groupings, you will better be able to detect and identify the things that repeatedly trigger your grief and pain.

TRIGGER #1: PEOPLE

Each holiday season, I look forward to reading Christmas cards and letters. It's the only time of year I get caught up on all our friends and family.

When I was a little girl, my parents used to get the usual load of holiday Christmas cards each year. My mother always enjoyed hearing from everyone and would invariably pass along the updates to each of us. It was an annual tradition.

But there was one letter, from one family that got special attention in our home. It's what became known as the annual brag letter. We loved it because it always left us in hysterics. You wouldn't believe the creative ways they found to boast about themselves. Each page oozed with trips, promotions, awards, and honors. Their photo was perfect, usually on a beach at a resort, and their tans looked as if they had been painted on. It was amazing that a simple stamp could transport such hefty accolades.

Apparently the honor of receiving an annual brag letter has been passed down to the next generation, because my husband and I now get one too. Filled with the same fluff and pomp, we read the letter each year with rolling eyes, which is quite a trick. It's been over fifteen years and the letters continue to come. As pride would have it, they get worse each year. Evidently no one has had the nerve to tell them how bad their letters are, so they continue in the tradition.

But an interesting thing has happened to me over the years. What I once found funny, as a kid, is no longer amusing as an adult. Life for us is hard, and I am reminded of it daily. Unable to do many things we would love to do because of Dani's disabilities, our lives have numerous restrictions that no one else could possibly imagine. Bloating brag letters that boast of all this family claims to do and accomplish, only reminds me of what we cannot do all the more.

To be fair, let me say that I'm convinced this family has never wished to make anyone feel bad. Clearly they brag for their own benefit. But it is one of those things that can trigger great grief in me if I don't keep close tabs on it.

Each Christmas I would open their letter, read it, and then sit down and have a good cry. Every year their children were cuter, smarter, stronger, and more active. They made more money, took more trips, and bought new cars. They seemed to have it all. While we, on the other hand, lived paycheck-to-paycheck: paying medical bills, going to doctors, just trying to survive.

After many years of repeatedly walking onto the same landmine, I finally decided to quit reading the brag letter altogether. And what do you know… my holidays are much better now. Choosing to spare myself the unnecessary pain, I now simply file their unopened letter with the others. Why? Because, that is what's best for my own welfare.

Why subject myself to a landmine that I know will go off every time I step on it? Reading their letter doesn't edify my life in any way, it in fact holds an impeccable record of pulling me down. Refusing to read it is my way of watching where I walk, and it's working quite well.

To be honest, I don't feel this Christmas letter is a bomb for me any longer. I know this family isn't all they say they are. It isn't possible. I don't read the letters for a different reason now: the sheer fact that I enjoy exercising the power to protect myself. After all these years of being torn to bits, it feels real good!

People are bound to trigger emotions of grief inside us one way or another. Some do it unknowingly, some do it out of their own insecurities, and some do it simply because they are arrogant. All we can do is protect ourselves as best we can along the way.

Do you needlessly allow another person to trigger pain inside you? Do you repeatedly seek counsel from someone who is unsympathetic toward your situation? Unfortunately, sometimes we expect those closest to us to understand our situation, when in fact they do not. As a result they do more harm than good.

If this is your experience, distance yourself from them, at least with regards to your pain and grief. Few people grasp what it's like to be the parent of a disabled child. It's unreasonable to expect someone who is not in your shoes to know what you are going through. Have a little mercy on them, and on yourself, and seek the counsel of one who understands. Talk to a fellow parent who knows what you are going through, but most of all talk to God. He is the only one who truly knows and understands what you are going through. He is waiting to help you as well.

TRIGGER #2: SITUATIONS

"Finally, I am going to let her do it. Maybe she'll do okay and actually have fun like all the other kids. What's the worst thing that could happen? I am right here with her, and I can see her nearly every second. Besides, what a nice break it would be to sit and rest while she plays."

Nice thought, but never again! At eight years old I thought, maybe, Dani could play like the other kids in the tunnels at the local fast food restaurant. For some odd reason I felt rather bold that day as I rationalized to myself that things were different now that she was a little older.

In the past she would go into the maze and never come out, which was always a nightmare. But, this time I clung to a faint hope that things would be different. I had no basis for this hope, but I had it anyway. I'm still not sure what I was thinking at the time.

So, on the wings of my own well wishing, up she went into the vast tunnel system of the restaurant. The clock began to tick in my head. Forty long minutes passed and she had still not come back down. On a rare occasion I'd see the whites of her eyes as she gazed out one of the Plexiglas holes, then off she'd disappear to who knows where.

Whenever our eyes did met, I'd enthusiastically sign for her to come down, but she'd simply drift away as if blind to my call. Clearly I had made a big mistake in letting her go up there.

I began to get nervous as the other mothers and children started trickling out the door. Like hens gathering their cooperative chicks, women and children paired up with ease and walked out to their cars. While my Autistic baby bird remained in the tunnels, completely unaware of the time.

In desperation I asked one of the last remaining girls to help me retrieve my daughter. In a flash she presented me with my little chick, now safe and sound, back on the ground. I was relieved beyond words to have her back in my arms again. Only the smell of her poopy pants changed my mood, prompting me to vow I would never allow her to go up into any tunnel system ever again. It's an oath still fresh and active in our lives today.

My hope for a sense of normalcy that day at the restaurant failed yet again. Seeing the playground and all the other mothers with their children looked so tempting I couldn't resist. I wanted to give it just one more try. So, I threw caution to the wind, only to have it blow back at me with the foulest of odors.

In the tunnels that day, feeling sad and defeated, I was once again reminded of all our many limitations and restrictions. Even the littlest of things can be impossible for our little girl, and that will never change. Sometimes it is difficult to accept.

Nearly everywhere we go we're met with reminders of what she cannot do and will never be: the local playground, the grocery store, baby showers, birthday parties, sleepovers. Even a trip to the library is a reminder of her severe delay in development. Almost anything can prompt the sad reality that our child is not like others.

I wonder what situations serve to trigger your grief? Do you find yourself wishing that your boy could play baseball as you drive past the busy baseball fields? Does your mind go idle as you watch the neighborhood children run, play, and have fun? Maybe it's something as simple as a child's picture on a coworker's desk or a walk past the nursery door at church.

Potentially painful situations are all around us, and like landmines, they have the capacity to trigger tremendous episodes of grief. No matter what we do, grief will be triggered one way or another. Since this is true, it's wise to buffer ourselves whenever possible.

If it takes not opening a Christmas letter, then don't open it. Do what you have to do to protect yourself. Feeling more pain won't speed up the grieving process, it'll just make the journey more painful.

Pay attention to the things that trigger your pain, then work around it. Odds are, further down the line, it will no longer have the powerful impact it once had.

TRIGGER #3: PERSONAL WEAKNESSES

Have you ever taken the time to identify your personal weaknesses? Can you name three things that qualify as kinks in your armor? What is it that typically brings you down? Is it an issue with pride, self-pity, critical thoughts, negative speech, denial, or lack of faith?

If you are having trouble going to such a tender spot, allow me to be the guinea pig. Perhaps seeing my weaknesses will help you find your own.

Okay, here goes. By far the biggest weaknesses I battle are those of negative thoughts and poor self-esteem. They have been my enemies for as far back as I can recall. Having never been told I was inferior, or abused in any way, I've come to understand that these inborn weaknesses are fueled by two primary things: Satan's strategic plan to use them to bring me down, and my inability to identify them in the first place. This is why identifying our kinks is so important. It's half the battle!

Like any trial, Dani's disabilities challenged these weaknesses like nothing had ever done before. As if hopping into the driver's seat, they began to dominate my life.

Consumed with negative thoughts, my insecurities began to mount until I was nothing but doom and gloom walking around on two legs. Depressing thoughts haunted me constantly saying, *"She isn't what I wanted" "Life will never be the same"* and

"I'll never be happy again." Rarely did a positive thought enter my head.

With negative thoughts and poor self-esteem as my constant companions, I was a miserable soul. Destined for a life of misery, it was time for a little soul searching and subsequent cleaning. Philippians 4:8 helped me do just that:

"Finally, brothers, whatever is true, whatever is noble, whatever is right, whatever is pure, whatever is lovely, whatever is admirable — if anything is excellent or praiseworthy — think about such things."

It was time to admit my weaknesses and shore them up. I was losing the battle, and I needed a defense. Paul's letter to the Philippians did the trick. Any thought that was not noble, right, pure, lovely, admirable, or praiseworthy, had to go. No more weak links. I needed the power of God!

Since those early years, I've worked diligently to train myself to take captive every thought (2 Corinthians 10:5). It wasn't natural at first, but soon I learned how to measure all my thoughts and attitudes against those that are godly in Philippians 4:8. And the good news is --- it really works!

Personal weaknesses are like the wizard of Oz. Remember the guy behind the curtain who turned all the thingamabobs and flipped all those gadgets? He projected a frightening and powerful image when he, in fact, was nothing more than a man. Everyone was under his power and control, until he was exposed for who he really was. The same is true when it comes to our own personal flaws: once exposed they are much less powerful.

If you are not sure what your weaknesses are, I encourage you to do some soul searching. It can be a real eye-opener! Knowing what our weaknesses are gives us the upper hand by letting us know what to look for and where to guard ourselves. Personal weaknesses are nothing but little faults that limit our potential. Once exposed and then reinforced, these cracks can actually make us stronger in the end.

Take the time to evaluate what pulls you down and holds you back, and then give it to God. He is your Creator and He wants to help you overcome any weaknesses you may have. Trust Him to do a good work in you. He will!

CHAPTER FOUR

Goals of Grief

Once we are able to see our grief for what it is, determine to let it change us for the better, and accept the fact that many people around us will never understand all we face as parents of disabled children, it's time to set some goals.

Without goals in life we flounder about aimlessly, achieving nothing in the process. It is natural to have specific ambitions when it comes to our education, jobs, and finances, but seldom do we set goals for our pain. When was the last time you asked your self, *"What is my ultimate objective with regards to this pain in my life? Where do I want it to take me? What kind of person do I want it to help me become?"* Rare is the person who dares go into these uncharted waters.

But you and I must determine to go there, because if we don't, we will wander about aimlessly in a sea of grief for the rest of our lives. This is not to say we can't learn to cope. Many families learn to cope with disabilities. It simply means that without goals for our grief, we will never experience the true freedom that lies beyond merely muddling our way through. God has a better plan for you and I: therefore, we must make His plan our goal. This is our key to true liberty.

So what are our options? If we can't have what we truly want, restoration of our child, what should be our objective? I believe as special parents we should set our sights on four distinct goals, each of great importance.

GOAL #1: MOVE THROUGH ALL FIVE STAGES OF GRIEF

Grief consists of five phases: denial, anger, bargaining, depression and acceptance. All five stages are important and serve a vital purpose in our ability to move beyond the point of grief. As if tackling our pain from every conceivable angle, each stage works in its own special way to bring about greater healing. Walking through only a few stages or permanently residing in one or two, on the other hand, only leads us to never-ending sorrow and sadness.

It's important to be aware of these five phases, and determine to move through them, but this isn't all we need to know. Equally as important is the knowledge that passing through each stage *once* is never enough. We are all bound to revisit them over and over again, and it is alright to do so.

Determining to move through all phases of grief does not mean you will go through each stage only once, it simply means you will not allow yourself to get stuck in one or two and neglect the others. Vacillating between anger, bargaining, and depression is not a healthy response to grief, neither is complete denial. Only when we walk through all five stages, in their entirety, will true healing be found. This is why we must pass through them all.

One of the least visited, and most misunderstood, phases of grief is that of acceptance. For some reason nearly all of us gravitate toward the other stages, while neglecting the last one that is so vital. I am not sure why we do this, but let's expose the facts so we can overcome the problem.

The biggest misconception we have when it comes to acceptance is in believing that once we enter this phase we are done with grief altogether. After all, it is listed last and it is called acceptance, inferring it's the end of the line with regards to our grief.

But, reaching the point of acceptance doesn't necessarily mean we are anywhere near completing our voyage. As much as I wish it were this easy, this has not been my experience. Acceptance for me has come in small increments over the years, not one lump all at once. It's been a difficult soul-searching journey that, at times, I've had to deliberately walk.

Much of grief's scenery has been cyclic in nature. I have been angry countless times, I've sought to block out the pain through denial on numerous occasions, and I suffered great depression more than I care to recall. In the end I've come to understand that the five stages of grief are not places we are to visit only once, but places we often need to visit several times.

Cycling through all five stages is not only common, but also perfectly normal. Please don't ever let anyone, including yourself, make you believe you should move through all five stages then suddenly come out a whole new person. Allow yourself the right to visit each phase, as many times as you need to; it's perfectly normal. Just don't permit yourself to get stuck in one or two phases.

Perhaps the temptation to continually recycle through the first four stages of grief is because they are like an opened wound. They hurt and bring great distress whenever touched; therefore we focus on them the most. The fifth stage of acceptance, however, is a little different. It doesn't scream at us like the others, and in turn gets less attention. This does not diminish its vital role in healing, however. Like a medicated cream, this fifth stage brings about final restoration by coating the other stages like a healing salve.

Without acceptance, denial, anger, bargaining, and depression bring nothing but heartache. No mending or growth will ever be achieved when we fail to move beyond their bounds. But life begins to change when we choose to apply acceptance to our wounds. Like the many layers of a scar, each time we complete all five stages of grief, we come out with a greater degree of healing.

The evidence of our wounds is still clear for all to see, our lives will confirm their existence, but in the end we come out stronger, healthier, and better able to carry out the plan God has for our lives.

Determine to move through all five stages of grief. It is your only way to true and lasting healing.

GOAL #2: GIVE YOUR PAIN TO GOD

When was the last time you gave God your pain? Have you ever wrapped it all up and simply laid it at His feet? I have many times; the problem is I always take it back. Forgetting God wants me to give it all to Him, I take it all back and resume as if I had never handed it to Him in the first place.

I've often wondered why God doesn't just remove the pain from my life. It seems we'd all be better off. I would be happy, God wouldn't have to hear me fuss all the time, and those around me would surely reap great things from my bettered condition.

But God doesn't work that way. His plans go far beyond our own. While we want immediate relief, He seeks to refine us and bless us in a permanent way. As you might guess, His work on us requires that we be refined, and this of course is never easy or comfortable.

Pain is like a scalpel. It cuts to the very core in order to excise that which needs to be removed. Since sin and selfishness are the pervasive cancer common to all mankind, it is no wonder that God allows the pain in our lives to rid us of this terminal disease.

When you can't get what you want, it inflicts terrible pain. In our duress we are tried and tested in a way that reveals who we really are like nothing else can. For this very reason, it is very valuable and should not be avoided. Though none of us relish the thought of having to endure pain and heartache, they serve to enrich our lives, ultimately improving us in the end.

There isn't one great man or woman of the Bible who didn't suffer great sorrow, grief and despair. Even the sinless perfect Lamb of God, Jesus Christ, suffered for sins He did not commit. Why should we be any different? He didn't suffer in order to become a better person. As God in the flesh, He endured so that He could sympathize with our suffering (Hebrews 4:15).

Getting rid of the pain in our lives should never be our primary goal, for then our focus is on ourselves and not on God. Setting our sights on God, giving Him all of our praise and honor, then giving Him all that hurts our hearts, should be our ultimate goal. He not only can handle it, but He wants to!

GOAL #3: KEEP THE FAITH

Webster's Dictionary defines faith as having a complete trust or confidence in someone or something. The Bible defines faith as, *"being sure of what we hope for and certain of what we do not see"* (Hebrews 11:1 NIV).

Both define faith as a confident and sure trust in something or someone, but the Bible adds greater clarity to the meaning of faith by describing it as having confidence in that which we cannot see.

If you've ever been tempted to lose your faith, you know how scary it can be. It's frightening because our faith supports the very foundation on which we stand. The King James Bible says, *"faith is the substance of things hoped for, the evidence of things not seen."* This word *substance* means support or foundation. Like an earthquake, when our faith begins to quiver, it can be absolutely terrifying.

I used to think that only difficult situations challenged our faith. I've come to believe that our faith is put to the test every single day. If I am having a good day, do I think of God or stay in my happy zone, not giving Him a second thought? On the other hand, if I'm having a terrible day, do I try to handle it all myself and risk having a melt down, or do I give my problems to God? Either way my faith is put to the test.

That is why it is important to pay careful attention to the condition of our faith. If it is weak and failing, we need to be able to identify it and take the proper actions to nurse it back to health. Over the past nineteen years my faith has been tried and tested in every imaginable way. I've taken notes on my journey and come up with four things we should know when it comes to our faith.

First, it is only by faith we can please God (Hebrews 11:6). It doesn't matter what we say, do, or intend to do, nothing but pure unadulterated faith can please God.

As one who knows the inner most parts of our hearts, He knows the kind of faith we hold deep inside. He knows if our foundation is strong or weak, if it looks good but is in fact corrupt at the core, or if it is perhaps as small as a mustard seed, but ready to bloom into a beautiful tree.

True faith, no matter how big or small, pleases God and has the potential to do many great things. It is simple, straightforward, and the only thing we will ever do that can please the heart of God.

Second, faith is the only thing that grants us righteousness (Genesis 15:6). Since we've all sinned and fallen short of the glory of God (Romans 3:23), no one is clean in His eyes. Because of this, we cannot even come close to Him, let alone experience intimacy with Him.

But through faith in Jesus we are cleansed of our sins and given permission to draw near to the very heart of God. Simple, child-like faith is all we need to approach His holy throne. No amount of work or good intentions can cleanse us from our sins; only our complete trust in Christ can please the Father. It's that simple.

Third, it's important to understand that faith is not a thing; it is a process. Believing faith is only that which gets us into heaven limits all the possibilities it truly holds. As a result, what was meant to be a great and mighty foundation, designed to support us through the worst of trials, is instead flimsy and frail.

To believe faith is only a thing we need to receive eternal life is true, but incomplete. As a process, faith is a journey that lasts a lifetime. As we walk with God, each step serves to increase our confidence, build our endurance and deepen our trust in Him. The temptation to shrink back and give up when times get tough becomes less, while a greater devotion to Him begins to grow. A cleansing faith that pleases the heart of God is a process designed for us to walk every day of our lives.

Last but not least, our faith is often mixed with doubt. Now this may sound like a contradiction, but it's not. Knowing that faith is a process naturally implies areas of deficit. As we leave these degrees of lesser faith behind, we move forward to a greater faith, hence the term process.

The father of a boy afflicted with an evil spirit that causes him to repeatedly injure himself and attempt suicide, understood this concept of faith amazingly well. After the disciples' failed attempt to heal his boy, the father went to Jesus. Describing his son's sufferings, he asked Jesus to heal him, but in a doubting kind of way. He said, *"if you can do anything, take pity on us and help us"* (Mark 9:22).

Things were going well till the father used the word *"if"*. Then, like a burst balloon, his doubt was exposed. " *'If you can'?"* said Jesus. *"Everything is possible for him who believes"* (Mark 9:23). Why such a stern response to a two-letter word? Because even a seed of doubt will weaken our faith, ultimately hindering our spiritual development.

Interestingly enough, though this desperate father experienced doubt, he was not reprimanded for it. Instead, Jesus pointed it out in no uncertain terms. Once his weakness was exposed the father exclaimed, *"I do believe; help me overcome my unbelief!"* and without question, his plea deeply touched the heart of Jesus. After all, this is just the kind of faith that pleases Him so very much!

Do you feel like the desperate father of this severely afflicted boy? Have you gone to Jesus asking for His help, only to find doubt holding you back?

Doubt does to a Christian what kryptonite does to Superman. It weakens even the strongest believer. Imagine how it thwarts the spiritual growth of a new believer. Disbelief is a treacherous obstacle in the life of any believer and one that we should seek to rid ourselves of completely.

Confess any doubts you may have of God and what He can do for you, then ask Him to give you a greater measure of faith. Faith is a gift from God (1 Corinthians 12:9) and one He wants to give you freely. Shore up your foundation by increasing faith, and then you'll be amazed how your walk with Him will begin to change.

GOAL #4: DEVELOP AN ATTITUDE OF GRATITUDE

Question: Where do you find a turtle with no legs? *Answer*: Right where you left it. It's corny but symbolic of many who are at a standstill in grief. Like turtles in their shells, they recoil from the world and refuse to move on. It is sad, less than honorable, and not what we should ever desire to be.

The other day I was taking our daughter to a park for a walk. As we approached the park I saw a turtle in the middle of the road. My blood pressure began to rise as a fear for his survival began to brew. Slow and methodical, like an old grandfather clock, he ticked along at a set speed no one but God could alter.

I parked the car then hustled over to the turtle. Arriving safe and sound on the side of the road, I pointed my finger into the gutter and said to Dani, *"Look! There's a turtle! Isn't he the cutest little guy in the world?"*

Though not a fan of reptiles, I admired that little turtle in the trench. As a human I have never dreamed of walking across the road in such a slow fashion for fear I would surely die. But he was doing the best he could and as a result, his tenacity caught my eye. To me at that moment, he *was* the cutest little guy in the world.

If you were a turtle what kind would you be? Would you be stuck in your shell hidden from society, or out and about mingling with the world? Would you be withdrawn into your small world focusing on all your problems, or looking beyond your circumstances to see the world around you?

True happiness will always remain an elusive dream to those who keep their eyes on themselves, because inner joy is never found within ourselves. It comes from having a mind that is set on things that are beyond self.

By nature, grief focuses on itself. It feels pain and turns inwardly as a result. While it serves the valuable purpose of identifying a need, failing to move past it always leaves us immobile on the side of the road.

Since grief prompts us to look inward, we must determine to look outward, beyond ourselves. The question is how do we do this?

The key is simple. Develop an attitude of gratitude! Count your blessings and thank God for every one of them. You *are* blessed, you know. It's easy to count our problems, but I challenge you to itemize every one of your blessings.

Even when life is hitting you the hardest, there are good things worth noting. With the right mind-set, even the darkest days won't be able to mask what God has done for you.

I once had a job as a school nurse. I had no office, no phone, and no desk. Each morning after checking all the children's backpacks for notes from parents, I would open my briefcase in the lunchroom and begin to do my work. Two hours later I would pack up my things and begin to prepare lunch for 85 students. I hated that job because I did everything but nursing. Our need for the money outweighed my distaste for the job, so I continued to do what I didn't want to do.

At first I worked at that job like a turtle in my shell. Focusing on all its bad points, I was miserable. One day Jimmy heard me complaining and tapped on my shell. Popping my head out to hear what he had to say, he promptly advised me to develop an attitude of gratitude. *"Count your blessings"* he said, *"Even if they are smaller than small."*

I took his advice and began to write them all down. One by one, petty as they were, I documented every conceivable blessing I could come up with.

As if striking me between the eyes, light began to dawn on the crux of my problem. Suddenly I knew why I had pulled into my shell and was so miserable. It was my own selfish pride.

As a nurse I wanted to care for the children, not be a lunch time cook. I wanted an office, a desk, and a phone of my own. Convinced I was the only school nurse in the world who not only didn't have an office, but was in fact a lunch lady, it was more than I could bear. Focusing entirely on myself, I was miserable, just as a turtle inside her shell should be.

However, when I began to look beyond myself and count my blessings, things miraculously began to get better. I was still Nancy Douglas RN/Lunch Lady, but now I had an attitude of gratitude. I had a job, it paid the bills, and I was helping to feed 85 disabled children who could not otherwise feed themselves.

Believe it or not, it turned out to be one of the best jobs I ever had, for it coaxed me out of my shell by forcing me to look beyond myself. It made me do what I didn't want to do and stretched me in a way I had never been stretched before. Before I knew it, I was happy and content doing what I would never otherwise have chosen to do.

Has grief taken its toll on you? Are you at a standstill, unable to move on? God has before you a great and mighty plan and bondage to grief is not part of it. See your pain for what it truly is, then determine to move forward. Allow your heartache to lead you closer to the heart of God, and begin looking for the things that trigger your grief. Above all, set positive goals for your pain and keep your eyes on God.

Believe it or not, I still feel the sting of heartache even after nineteen years, but I've traveled this road long enough to know that it's all right to feel my sorrow. I don't have to deny the pain or come up with an answer this very moment. I can simply feel the sadness and all that goes with it, then pick myself up by the bootstraps, determine to remain positive, and move forward.

Did you know that even your most trying days can bring renewed hope? They really can. I have literally had days that were so bad they convinced me the next *had* to be better. And it always is.

The moral of the story is...never, ever give up. We can't avoid or remove the pain life dishes out to us, but we can have an attitude of gratitude. Your grief is not too much for Him to bear. He seeks to carry your burdens and is waiting for you to come to Him now. Go to Him and give him all your sorrow, heartache, and sadness.

CHAPTER FIVE

Marriage

Over half of all marriages end in divorce, and the divorce rate among parents with disabled children is as high as 80%. With every marriage facing disturbing odds of survival, the marriage with a special needs child faces even more daunting probabilities.

My husband and I have been married for 24 years and so far beaten the initial 50% chance of failure, but that's not all we've had to overcome. According to additional statistics that apply to our marriage, we risk an 80% chance of divorce due to Dani's disabilities and another 85% chance of collapse due to Jimmy's full time job traveling as a consultant. Now, I am not a statistician, but am I right? Could our marriage have a 215% chance of failure? Is that even possible?

As ominous as it sounds, I am not worried about our relationship. After all these years, I think we are going to make it. We've been through a lot in our years together, and it's been a rough ride at times, but to this day we are the best of friends. There is no one in the world I would rather be with than my companion, advisor, confidant, and true love. He is a gift from God whom I value and admire with all my heart.

Our marriage has been put to the test on some of the deepest possible levels. We've had to learn to work together through financial difficulties, goal setting, future planning, career decisions, child rearing, personal grief, and the raising of a special needs child. Not only have we had to work together to successfully handle these issues, we've had to maintain a strong and healthy marriage in the midst of it all. It's a tricky balancing act that can easily go wrong, which is why this chapter is so important to those of us facing these challenging odds.

As I look at marriages falling apart all around us, I can't help but ask myself: *What is so bad that it's driving them to divorce? How could it be worse than having a disabled child?* I say this because the couples I see bailing out nearly always have a larger home, their children are healthy, normal and active, their husbands do not travel full-time, and their lives have not been devastated with disability. For the most part they appear free as birds with full lives at their fingertips. Their inability to survive boggles my mind.

Why do other marriages fail while ours has remained intact? In the past, when my husband and I would discuss this puzzling phenomenon, I'd say, "*I just don't understand why so many people are getting divorced. Marriage isn't that hard; it isn't for us anyway.*" To which he'd promptly reply, "*But, it isn't easy dear, we work very hard in our marriage and it hasn't just happened, it's been a lot of diligent work on our part.*"

For years I never understood his theory. I believed our marriage was chalked up to compatibility. We were the perfect fit, and that was the reason for our success. Somehow in our ignorant young years we allowed the Holy Spirit to guide us together and the rest is history. We were simply made for each other, like two peas in a pod.

My hypothesis, however, has weakened over the years. Jimmy and I are actually two very different people. He is an eternal optimist and I'm a professional pessimist. His food has to be as hot and spicy as his palate can handle, while I prefer a more bland country style cooking. He runs hot, I run cold. I like all the lights on in the house and he prefers just enough to see what he's doing. He is content with little, while I battle the relentless desire to have more. We are in fact two very different peas that happen to live in the same pod, yet it works.

I don't know all the reasons behind the divorces that cripple society. I don't fully understand why our marriage has thrived either, but what I do know I gladly share with you. This chapter is a synopsis of things I've learned are invaluable lifesavers in our marriage. I believe they are the reasons why we've been able to beat such incredible odds.

For starters, let me share with you one very important truth. Any marriage can survive, no matter what it's up against. Even a marriage on life support, with only days to live, can be resuscitated. I know this because I've seen it happen. No marriage *has* to die, it's a choice made by one or both partners.

It goes against popular belief, but believe it or not, circumstances do not determine the outcome of a marriage, people do. External circumstances are simply misplaced labels. Marital success isn't a matter of what happens to us, what we have, or what we do not have. It depends on the character of the two joined together and the goals each have set.

If two partners make it their ambition to remain married and implement the following key elements into their partnership, their marriage will not be destroyed. Divorce will not be an option no matter what comes their way, and they will succeed even in the midst of life's most trying situations. I pray your marriage not only survives but also thrives.

MARRIAGE LIFESAVER #1: RESPECT

The fastest and most effective way to erode any human bond is to show contempt. From subtle underestimation to blatant disregard, disrespect is a corrosive force guaranteed to dissolve any relationship no matter whose it is, or how long it has been in place.

Simply put, respect means to "hold in high value." It involves putting someone or something before yourself, thinking of them before you think of yourself, and placing their value above your own. It is a selfless attitude that challenges our pride like nothing else can.

In the instance of marriage, respect must be present and active in three distinct areas: respect for God, respect for your spouse, and respect for each of your children. Like a cord of three strands, this reverent trio makes a marriage impermeable to the enemy. But just one link, when weakened, will threaten the integrity of the marriage.

RESPECT GOD

The first commandment God gave Moses said, *"You shall have no other gods before me"* (Exodus 20:3). Having led His people out of slavery, God wasted no time in giving them ten instructions to live by, the first of which was to hold Him high above all things.

God wanted only what was best for the nation of Israel. They were His people, set apart from all other nations, and He wanted to bless them beyond measure in order to glorify His name. All they had to do was put Him first in their heart and minds; a simple instruction that proved to be the most difficult one to carry out.

With hearts forever longing to be like the pagan nations around them, keeping God on the throne of their hearts was their number one stumbling block. Continually drifting from their

Creator and Lord, they broke this first command over and over again. As a result, their lives were a never-ending cycle of failure, repentance, and punishment.

As frustrating as their repeated failures are to read, we are no different today than the nation of Israel was back then. Placing God on the throne of our hearts, and keeping Him there, is our most challenging obstacle as well. It is a problem common to all mankind; no matter what moment of history in which we live.

God listed this command as the first of ten for two reasons. It is to be our highest priority, and it is the most difficult one to carry out. With this in mind, our primary goal should be to work diligently to keep it. To do so ensures we receive His blessing and not His curses.

So where do we begin? How do we honor God's highest but most difficult command to keep? An excellent way to start is by learning from the past. It nearly always insures a better tomorrow. There is no better way to learn than from God's own people and the mistakes they made in order to see how we can succeed in putting Him first in our own lives today.

There is a trend in the Old Testament. Every time the Israelites turned their backs on God it was when they were challenged in two areas: time and trials. If God took too long to accomplish something, they began to waver and if the fire of circumstance began to get too hot, they would invariably turn and head in a new direction. In either case their dedication to

Him would weaken and their faith would begin to falter, and soon they were turning away from the One who loved them most. Invariably, when disaster would strike, they would call on Him in distress and the cycle would begin again.

In a moment's time their eyes would drift from God, and the ground beneath their feet would begin to crumble. With doubt establishing a foothold in their heart, their faith would begin to erode, as God slipped off the throne of their heart. Selfish things of the world soon took His place as their respect for Him began to fade.

As you gaze through this window of history, do you see your own reflection in the glass? How committed are you to God? When the going gets tough where do you place your trust? Who is on the throne of your heart when the clock ticks away and it's clear you aren't going to get what you want? Do you begin to drift from your faith and take matters into your own hands?

God is our Creator and Christ His son is our Savior, no one deserves our reverence more. Only by putting our trust in the Lord will we succeed against great odds. Perfect and holy, they live beyond the bounds of time, know all things past, present, and future, and seek only that which is best for us. Without respect and undying commitment to Him, all things in life will eventually crumble and fall.

But with God all things are possible. If God is for us, who can be against us? (Romans 8:31) Even in times of great distress

He is our strength and salvation (Isaiah 33:2). He is our defense, even when we sin (1 John 2:1) and because of this, deserves our utmost honor and respect. An undying reverence to God should be our number one priority.

RESPECT YOUR SPOUSE

When was the last time you heard someone badmouth his or her spouse? They criticized their intelligence, critiqued their appearance, or condemned the way they did something. Like a high-powered rifle, they used words as ammunition to shoot down their partner every chance they could get. Some couples thrive on pointing out the faults of the one they chose, in spite of the damage it causes; it's a sport they thoroughly enjoy year-round.

Early on in our marriage there were many things my husband committed to do, one of which was to never speak an unkind word about me to anyone, in or out of my presence. Since I am far from perfect, he no doubt has had to bite his tongue on countless occasions. To my knowledge he has successfully lived by this motto our entire marriage, and I have done the same for him.

What we say about our partners is a reflection of our respect for them. If you speak negatively about your spouse you *are* eroding the foundation of your marriage, there are no two ways about it. No matter how you label them careless words that hurt and devalue your partner never go unnoticed and will always work against your relationship.

This is not to say constructive criticism does not have its place. We all need outside input on how to better ourselves, but it's always done with great love and compassion, never with venomous words designed to hurt and demean. Know the difference between constructive criticism and blatant disrespect and exercise only that which lifts up your husband or wife.

One of the most neglected areas of respect we as parents of disabled children can have toward one another is in the area of grief. Do you respect the way your partner grieves or do you find yourself telling them how they should feel and when they should be done? This critical eye, especially in such a painful area, can wreak havoc on a relationship, since it is a gross form of disrespect.

I learned this lesson firsthand from my husband. As one who had a more difficult time accepting my role as a parent to a special needs child, I was not an easy person to live with for years. I cried, fought with God, questioned Him, and battled life as a whole on a daily basis. In the midst of it all, Jimmy had to not only handle his own grief, but watch and live with the turmoil I was going through as well.

One day, when I was extremely angry with God, I spoke my mind. Unable to understand how a God who loved us so much would not take this pain from our family. I tearfully asked Jimmy if he ever got mad at God too.

Unruffled he replied, *"No, I don't get mad at God. I figure He knows what He is doing and I don't question Him. Your anger toward God is between you and God. It has nothing to do with me."*

His response was amazing. At that moment the priceless value of respect for another's grief was not only revealed but also extended to me, and it felt great. Though he had never been angry with God he didn't pass judgment on me. As a result, I was allowed to walk through my own personal grief, leaving our marriage uncompromised.

Do you think highly of your spouse or do you criticize him or her at every turn? Is your time spent analyzing faults or seeking ways to encourage? Far too many marriages are completely void of honor between partners. If this is true in your marriage, be the first to make a change. Respect your spouse by looking for ways to build them up. Show mercy when you do not understand their behavior, and determine to hold them in high esteem, even if you do not get it in return.

After you've done all this, pray! Pray for your marriage, your partner, yourself, and your children. Value their welfare above your own. In so doing, you will lay the second critical foundation for a strong and healthy marriage.

RESPECT YOUR CHILD

There used to be a saying *"God don't make junk."* The grammar may be poor, but it expresses perfectly our third key element for a strong and vibrant marriage.

A strong cord cannot be braided with only two strands, but a third creates a bond that is nearly unbreakable. The same concept is true in marriage. It's futile for us to honor God and our spouse, but neglect our child. God loves our children far more than we will ever be able to love them and because of this, their status in the eyes of God is supreme. Our goal must be to do the same.

As the parent of a disabled child I've fought many dark battles deep within myself. In the midst of each skirmish I'd ask God a multitude of questions I'd never ask another soul. *"What value does our daughter hold in society? What is her purpose? And, what is my purpose? Surely it's more than just caring for a child who will never be productive in the world."*

Though tough to see on paper, they were unavoidable questions that plagued my mind. I believe we all ask similar questions deep within ourselves; only good etiquette keeps us from asking them out loud. So what do we do with such questions?

Honesty is truly the best policy, and I live by this credo. If I am angry, I tell God. If I am angry with God, I tell Him that too.

I don't worry about offending Him because He already knows how I feel. My only concern is that I approach Him with the deepest respect so He will listen to me, and I will be able to hear Him when He speaks.

Honesty with God is so important. Parenting a special needs child can be absolutely overwhelming. Special schools, therapies, equipment, constant care and attention keep us hard at work for many years, often till the day we die. In spite of all our efforts sometimes the results can be minimal, making it even more difficult to handle. Feeling lost in a myriad of tasks can leave us wondering: what is the value and purpose of our child and all we do for them. Sometimes it seems as though the workload far outweighs the rewards, leaving us with many unanswered questions.

All the questions I've asked God have been answered with great mercy and love. He'd listen to me cry on His shoulder, as I'd vent my feelings and ask Him about all the things I know nothing about. His patience and love have sustained me through the worst of times and have never ceased to amaze me.

But as One who knows my heart better than I know it myself, God has called me on the carpet many times. My loving Father saw that I needed an attitude adjustment, and didn't hesitate to bring it to light. One time in particular, His response to one of my questions was very stern. It caught me completely off guard and I've not forgotten it to this day. It was regarding an attitude of disrespect I had for my daughter.

I was driving down the highway talking with God. Speaking to Him as I normally do, I began asking questions. I wasn't angry or upset; in fact I was quite calm as I tossed my query His way. With relative ease I asked, *"What went wrong with Dani? Was it something at conception or was it a chemical in my system that brought about her disabilities?"*

In that instant I sensed a change in His demeanor. The mercy and love that had always been prominent, were now more subdued, replaced by approaching discipline. I can't explain it, but I could feel it coming. Just like when I was a kid.

I had stepped over a line, but I wasn't sure what line or how I had done it. Wasting no time, He began firing questions at me. With eyes staring at the road ahead, it felt as though I was in a courtroom on wheels and I was on the stand. Guilty of a crime I knew nothing of; it was no doubt about to be exposed.

"What went wrong? Do you think I was asleep when she was conceived? Do you think I did not know how she would turn out?

In two seconds He asked three questions that made me feel as though I had undergone an extensive cross-examination. Revealing my sin at its core I could not deny the truth. Without another word He left me to ponder my offense. Dazed from His accuracy, I was stunned to discover I did not honor my own daughter.

As *His* special creation and prized possession she is a work of art, not a mistake I am left to care for the rest of my life. He knew she would be Autistic, deaf, and Failure to Thrive, and He allowed it. With a plan that involves her disability, He works out His perfect will in our lives, therefore I must respect her for who she is exactly the way He created her to be.

Since that day in the car I have never again asked God what went wrong. I understand nothing can go wrong when God is in charge. He cannot make a mistake, and He does not make junk. Every individual is His prized possession and should be honored as such. A child with a disability, no matter the extent, is no exception.

Do you respect your child as they are? Or do you wonder what went wrong? Marriage partners, who honor God and one another, will always suffer if they do not respect their children, disabled or otherwise. Children are a gift from God and should be valued greatly. Anything less is an affront to the One who created them. In the end, when you dishonor your child, you disrespect God.

Respect God, honor your marriage, and hold each child in high esteem just as they are. This is the first step in saving the life of your marriage.

MARRIAGE LIFESAVER #2: TEAMWORK

"Though one may be overpowered, two can defend themselves. A cord of three strands is not quickly broken" (Ecclesiastes 4:12). Prudent are these words spoken by the wisest man who ever lived, King Solomon.

A cord of three strands…what a perfect image of marriage! With Christ at the head, a man and a woman whose eyes are fixed on Him will not easily fall. This image of a three-cord strand takes me back to elementary school where long thick ropes hung from the gymnasium ceiling. Woven, twisted, and tied at the ends, these ropes were not easily broken. They lasted for years on end and withstood countless climbs from the students. In the end they showed little wear, if any at all.

But what would happen if one of the three cords were to give way? Though comprising only 1/3 of its part as a whole, it would cause the entire structure to unravel. Suddenly its ability to carry out its purpose would be compromised, and soon it would be nothing but a liability.

Such is the case in marriage. Without teamwork, its structural integrity is compromised to the point where it's destined to fall apart. With defenses brought low, vulnerability becomes a major threat. Respect begins to fade and soon it's every man for himself as the foundation begins to crack under the strain.

If you have ever worked on a team with members who don't pull their own weight, you know how devastating it can be. All it takes is one person who refuses to pull his or her own load or who insists on being negative, and the success of the whole team is compromised.

This is precisely what happened when Moses sent twelve men to spy out the Promised Land. Abundance, prepared by God and ready to be conquered, was forfeited all because of ten naysayers. In the end it cost the Israelites 40 years and the lives of an entire generation, minus Joshua and Caleb.

Much the way Moses sent the men out to spy the land promised to them by God, we are called to team up and conquer a land set before us. He never hands it to us on a silver platter; we must conquer it by faith. This conquest requires a joint effort.

Unfortunately, many marriages today are hanging by a thread. Christ is not the head of the home and solidarity among partners is virtually nonexistent. Selfish pride, hurt feelings, and needless competition divide each member making it impossible to obtain that which God has waiting for them.

What is holding your marriage together? Are you, your spouse, and God bound together like a strong cord that cannot be easily broken? Or are you each a fragile thread blown by the wind? Perhaps the strain of disability is beginning to unravel your marital bond, and it feels as if you are near the end of your rope.

Dear fellow parent, God is the answer! As the creator of marriage, He is the glue that holds us together. He wants your marriage to be strong and is willing to make it possible, but you must want it too. As a member of the team you must fight to keep the promise you made before Him. Believe that He is on your side, trust that He will heal and restore your marriage, and then focus your heart on Him.

Envision a triangle with Christ at the top. You are on the bottom left corner, and your spouse is on the bottom right. When you and your partner fix your eyes on God and begin to move toward Him, the distance between you and your spouse begins to lessen. It's unavoidable and there is no way around it. When two married people draw near to God, they can't help but draw near to one another as well!

Teamwork, with God as your boss, is the only remedy for a failing marriage. Forget extraneous details that fog the picture, your task is simple: seek the Lord with all your heart and He will direct your path. In the end your marriage will thrive as never before, and you'll conquer land you never thought possible. So, saddle up the horses, come together as one, and head for God. You're bound to succeed.

MARRIAGE LIFESAVER #3: PERSEVERANCE

I was recently asked if my marriage to Jimmy has ever been near divorce. I gladly said no, but was unable to take credit for it. I give all the honor to my husband and his tenacious will to lead us through each and every trial. Like a bulldog, he has had to dig his heals into the ground on numerous occasions in order to keep us stable amidst the storms of life. I have only mimicked what I've observed to be highly effective over the years.

One thing I admire most about Jimmy is his ability to persevere. It's something I do not have by nature. I flit and fly from one thing to another, while he floats through the sea of life like an ocean liner with its compass fixed on one point. Nothing can stop his will to reach a goal, and I absolutely love this quality in him. I love it so much I've allowed it to rub off on me. As a result I flit and fly around a lot less these days.

A firm resolve is a fine quality to have. After all, where would the world be without perseverance? Would we have electricity, refrigeration or decaffeinated coffee? Would we have bug spray, bubble bath, or corrugated boxes? Without question, we would not; for these critical necessities and countless luxuries would be nothing but a fleeting fantasy if history's inventors had lacked precious perseverance.

When the chips are down, no one likes a quitter. As one wired to give up at the least resistance, even I don't admire a person who quits without putting up a good fight. Party poopers make it hard to play games, fulfill commitments, and complete important jobs because they are always jumping ship.

In a world where fast and easy is always the preferred approach, hard work in spite of the odds is an all-too-rare character trait. As annoying as they are, those who give up too soon are a dime a dozen, which is one reason I believe many of us fail to see the abundant blessing God has waiting for us.

Like unopened presents, quitters forfeit precious gifts designed specifically for them by giving up too soon. Seeking to escape the pain, they run to the closest thing that eases their discomfort, cheating themselves in the process. In the end they suffer the tragedy of underachievement, never having a clue of the great things God had in store for them.

Did you know God doesn't like party poopers either? Hebrews 10:36 is proof positive of this truth as He promises to bless only those who do not give up. *"You need to persevere so that when you have done the will of God, you will receive what he has promised"* (NIV).

Don't miss the fact that God does not promise to bless those who persevere in just anything. Can you imagine Him blessing those who persevere in sin? Never. He only promises to bless those who persevere in doing His will, and since He instituted the bonds of marriage it should not be taken lightly or given up on easily.

Marriage is an oath taken before God and should be honored as such. As a gift from God, it should be protected with ferocious tenacity and placed in highest regard. Without this reverent respect, it will surely begin to falter when the going gets tough.

Do you honor your marriage? Is it precious and valuable; a thing you treasure and admire? Before we got married my husband set a ground rule. He said, *"Nancy, once we are married you are not going to run home to your mother. Any fights we have we will be ironed out ourselves, and the word divorce will never be said in our home, not even in joking."*

When I heard his words I thought they were rather odd. It's not like it had ever been my nature to run to mother so I wasn't sure what prompted him to say this. But as the concept began to sink in, I realized God was giving me a heads up in the form of one warning and a choice.

The warning was that of rough waters ahead, which neither of us knew about at the time. Along with this warning, He gave me an opportunity to decide to do the right thing long before the choice would have to be made. By doing all this in advance, when the fire of life got hot I was able to reflect back on my commitment to Jimmy, stick by his side, and persevere through the trial.

In essence, God was encouraging me to always stick close to the ocean liner I was about to marry. He knew I'd be a lot safer in the storm with Jimmy at my side, than trying to weather the storms alone like a mosquito in a typhoon.

Our little premarital agreement, made in the car after a date, was one of the wisest things we've ever done. To this day, we never so much as joke about getting a divorce, and I believe it's one reason we've never quit, saving our marriage against such tremendously daunting odds.

You'd be surprised what you can do when you set your heart and mind to it. You'd be equally surprised to see what you can accomplish when you choose to persevere. The human will can handle anything when it adopts an attitude of unrelenting resolve and when we do, endurance and perseverance become godly character traits that lead us to never give up.

As a result, like a cord of three strands, we gain the ability to stand firm in the midst of great odds, party pooping becomes a thing of the past, we persevere through whatever comes our way, and we please the heart of God.

SINGLE PARENTS

Are you a single parent? If so, I commend you for reading this chapter. I would have been tempted to skip over it. But since you've read it I suppose you might be wondering if you can have the strength of a cord with three strands if you don't have a spouse.

If this is your situation, bless your heart. I wish I could put my arm around you and give you a big hug of encouragement. Some days are almost more than I can bear. I only imagine the things you face as a single parent.

Though I cannot relate to your situation entirely, there is one thing I know for sure, God is with you and has written Psalms 68:5 just for you. *"A father to the fatherless, a defender of widows, is God in his holy dwelling"* (Psalm 68:5).

God promises to defend the weak by fathering the fatherless and defending the widows. Those who must endure hardship alone are the very ones to whom He makes this special guarantee. As a single parent you are never alone or abandoned, for He is by your side leading you every step of the way. Keep your eyes on Him, follow Him in all your ways, and obey His every command. Then you will be blessed beyond measure.

Never give up and never give in. Trust in the Lord with all your heart, soul, and mind!

CHAPTER SIX

Siblings

"Why isn't my sister like everyone else's?" Drew cried as I put him to bed for the night. His first day at kindergarten had been a good one up until then.

Going to school for the first time exposed him to many new things, one of which was the harsh reality that our family was not like all the others. When other mothers came to pick up his fellow classmates, something was different about them, and it didn't take him long to pinpoint the difference. His sister was nothing like his friends' sisters or brothers.

A child who was nearly always happy, Drew caught me off guard with his tearful question, and for a moment I wasn't sure how to answer it. It was one I had asked myself countless times before, but to no avail. What could I possibly tell him?

Faithful to provide, God gave me the answer just in the nick of time. Like a recorder, I recited to Drew what God was saying to me, *"Honey, you were chosen. Chosen to be a special brother to your sister that no one else can be. Your friends weren't chosen because they don't have what it takes; only you have what it takes. That is why your sister is not like the others."*

In the time it took for me to speak these words, Drew's demeanor made a rapid turnabout. As quickly as they came, his tears began to dissipate. Feelings of being ostracized were replaced with a sense of pride and what at first appeared to be an adversity began to look more like a privilege. God's words brought great comfort to him and it changed his attitude for good.

Since that first day of kindergarten, Drew has accepted his role in the family very well. He fulfills his position to the best of his ability and has made his father and me very proud, but it hasn't diminished the cost he's had to pay. His placement in our family has cost him dearly, which is something that will never change.

As hard as we've tried to compensate for our limitations, there are many things Drew has never been able to do. I know there are countless other things he's never even asked to do, knowing how it would tax our family. Simply having a friend over, for instance, has proven to be difficult over the years. How do you explain to your friends the sounds she makes from her world of Autism, or the sight of turning around to see her suddenly undressed? Is it worth having a friend over when you must always watch for the bathroom light because your sister is likely to have another bout with diarrhea? With such uncomfortable sights, sounds, and smells, sometimes it just isn't worth it.

It's easy to give in to the disability. A simple thing like having a friend over can be so difficult it isn't worth doing. Over the years Jimmy and I hit a record low in the number of functions we've had in our home. It's simply not worth it on top of all we deal with regarding her disabilities. Time and again we've been homebound because of Dani's diarrhea, vomiting, or migraine headaches. In the end we do much less than we would otherwise like, which makes our world smaller and smaller over time.

Through it all Drew has never complained. While he is by no means perfect, he has adapted exceptionally well to his role in our family, and I believe it's because God revealed his calling to him early on. Knowing that he was chosen by God Himself to be Dani's special brother enabled him to fill shoes he might otherwise have abandoned; as a result the sibling rivalry has been minimal, enabling our family to cope relatively well as a whole.

Now in his 20's, Drew has a heart that has clearly been blessed with an extra measure of compassion and love due to the life God has chosen for him. He sees the needs of others as many cannot, and possesses a quality of kindness few young men his age ever acquire. His experience of sacrifice has made him the man he is today, proving beyond a shadow of a doubt that God knew exactly what He was doing all along.

SET APART NOT SET ASIDE

I am glad I was there the night Drew went to bed crying. It did me a world of good to tell him about his calling, for it served to remind me of my own as well. He hadn't been the only one at the school comparing our family to others. I, too, had seen mothers with their normal children, and it broke my heart. I didn't have to be at the school to see it either; I saw it all around me everywhere I went.

But now, armed with this knowledge that we were chosen, our situation didn't seem so dismal. Even though our situation hadn't changed a bit, simply knowing our lives had purpose and meaning changed our outlook in a profound way. As a result, we received renewed strength and hope; something we'd need in abundance in the years to come.

But what about those who are unaware they've been chosen? What about the siblings of disabled children who feel cheated, burdened, and afflicted? Can they, too, find hope and peace in their situation? Yes, they can and the good news is it's never too late.

Whether they're entering kindergarten or completing college, your children need to know they've been set apart by God Himself. Chosen for a vital and specific role, they have been strategically placed precisely where they are to do a job no one else can do. They have the specific gifts, talents, and strengths to do exactly what God has called them to do, they simply need to become aware they've been set apart for the task, not set aside.

It's difficult to be set apart when it's not our own idea. While we want to feel as though we're distinct and one of a kind, there's a tremendous overriding need to be accepted and respected even amidst our uniqueness. We want to stand out, but not too much. We want to blend in, but in a very different way. It's an intricate and sometimes exhausting juggling act.

For instance, I like my clothing to be modern and up-to-date. If it's age appropriate, the color looks good on me, and doesn't add weight to my frame; I'm likely to give it a try. I love clothes and enjoy seeing how many different outfits I can create with what I've got. Clothes that are distinct and different are especially appealing.

Having said that, I never want to be too unlike those around me. I want to be unique without being odd or out of place. I want my dress to be nice, but not over the top, which begs the question many of you might be thinking, *"Which do you want? To be different and stand out, or be like everyone else and fit in?"*

Some may claim you cannot have both, but I declare you can. People do it all the time. They look distinctly different, yet fit into society quite well. Then there are others who attempt to stand out, and do so like a sore thumb. Hence, the fine balance between fashion that is tasteful verses that which is tacky.

The prophet Jeremiah fought a similar battle; only it had nothing to do with his attire. Called by God to speak as a prophet to His people and do what no one else around him was called to do, he was overcome with fear. Wondering how he could ever fill such enormous shoes, he went so far as to deny his manhood by saying, *"I do not know how to speak; I am only a child"* (Jeremiah 1:6).

He may not have understood it at the time, but his excuses were an act of rebellion. Disbelief that God had a plan for his life, and was able to carry it out, stopped him dead in his tracks, leaving him so skeptical he claimed to be a child.

In order to alleviate his fears, God addressed Jeremiah's problem at its very core saying, *"Before I formed you in the womb I knew you, before you were born I set you apart; I appointed you as a prophet to the nations"* (Jeremiah 1:5).

God had made His decision. Jeremiah was the man for the job. Long before he was ever born, he was chosen to be God's mouthpiece to the people. Born with all the talent, skill, and ability he would ever need to do the task, all he had to do was accept the job, trust in God, and obey the call. But first he had to understand that he had been chosen.

Such power these words hold to those of us who question our call. For when we believe God does not makes mistakes and is in full control, we are strengthened to do whatever we are called to do. Suddenly that which appeared insurmountable becomes entirely possible, and what first looked dismal and oppressive is a privilege and honor. It's all in how we look at it, and it's always best to see things through the eyes of God.

Have you ever blessed your normal children with the understanding that they have been chosen? Do they know they are special in their own way or do they feel excluded and set aside?

How our children choose to feel about their role in the family is ultimately up to them, but as parents we must do all we can to help them see that their position in the family is no mistake. God does not make mistakes and He is in complete control. He has a plan for each member of the family just as he or she is, and seeks to do great things in their lives. Sharing this with your child is the greatest gift you will ever give them.

SIBLING RIVALRY

If your home has some degree of competition going on among its children, take heart: you are not alone. Sibling rivalry is nothing new. It goes as far back as the first family. The first parents who ever lived faced the first and worst case of jealousy among their children as they lost the life of one son to the hands of the other:

"Now Cain said to his brother Abel, "Let's go out to the field."
And while they were in the field, Cain attacked his brother Abel
and killed him" (Genesis 4:8 NIV).

Abel was a shepherd and Cain grew crops in the field. Each gave offerings to the Lord, but Cain failed to give his very best. When God showed favor on his brother Abel, great contention began to rise within Cain, making his heart burn with anger.

Confronting the issue head-on, the Lord went directly to Cain. Seeing his fury grow deeper and more intense, He said to him, *"Why are you angry? Why is your face downcast? If you do what is right, will you not be accepted? But if you do not do what is right, sin is crouching at your door; it desires to have you, but you must master it"* (Genesis 4:6-7 NIV).

What great love it takes to confront someone as the Lord did Cain. It's a difficult thing to do but must sometimes be done in order to redirect someone who has gotten off course. This is exactly what God did when He saw where Cain's anger was leading him. Going straight to the issue, He diagnosed this farmer's heart with uncanny accuracy and recorded it in His word for a very good reason.

This story of history's first instance of sibling rivalry is invaluable to us for two reasons. First, it lets us know we are not alone. All families experience rivalry among children, even the first family, and in some fashion this provides comfort.

This account also serves as superb guidance on how to handle this jealousy when it creeps into our home. In two succinct verses, God gives us four clear steps to take when dealing with sibling rivalry, and when implemented in our homes, they can help diffuse angst among siblings.

STEP #1 - ACKNOWLEDGE YOUR CHILD'S EMOTIONS

When God saw that Cain was angry, He went to him and asked why he was angry. He didn't brush it off as a phase or mood; He approached him with candor and addressed the issue. In doing so, He gave Cain the opportunity to better see his anger for what it really was and defuse it before it got out of hand.

There is immeasurable value in acknowledging our child's feelings. It validates them as an individual and gives them an opportunity to see themselves in a more objective fashion. It is also a powerful way to show them your respect.

Nothing is worse than feeling as though our feelings do not matter. It is insulting and frustrating, and parents do it to their children all the time. We avoid confrontation by chalking it up to a phase they are going through, and never meet the issue head on. As a result, the child is left alone to sort out and deal with their feelings.

I think it goes back to the old adage that children are to be seen and not heard. The theory that they are here to serve us, and not the other way around, contributes to the problem as well. Our children are human beings. They see, feel, and react to difficult situations the same as adults, only they cannot always express it in words. How they feel is more likely to come out in their actions.

Just as parents of disabled children need freedom to feel the wide range of emotions that come with grief and loss, so do the siblings. As members of the family, their lives have been altered greatly as well, and they deserve to have their emotions acknowledged and respected. This is the first step toward conquering opposition among the children in your home.

STEP #2 – PROVIDE GUIDANCE

The second thing God did for Cain was offer him direction. Emotions can do a good job of getting us off course. That's when we need someone who loves and cares for us enough to guide us back on track. This is precisely what God did with Cain. He encouraged Him to do what was right.

Notice this encounter did not include a big lecture. God didn't even go so far as to tell Cain what to do. He simply said, *"If you do what is right, will you not be accepted?"* No mention of what he had to do to be accepted. Why? Because Cain already knew. He knew exactly what he was doing wrong; the issue was his free will to not do what was right.

The same is true when it comes to our children. More often than not, they know right from wrong. The battle isn't so much they lack the knowledge; it's the inability to do what is right. This is where we come in. Like God did with Cain, once we acknowledge our child's feelings, we must encourage him or her to respond correctly.

This is why the Bible says, "*... encourage one another daily, as long as it is called Today, so that none of you may be hardened by sin's deceitfulness*" (Hebrews 3:13). This word *encourage* means to call near or invite. It's when we draw near to our child and say, "*I know you can do the right thing.*" Sometimes this is all it takes for him or her to turn around and head in the right direction.

Respond to your children's feelings and encourage them to do what is right. This is the second step toward snuffing out sibling rivalry.

STEP #3 – GIVE OUT A WARNING

Once God pointed out Cain's anger and encouraged him to do what was right, He uttered a warning, "*But if you do not do what is right, sin is crouching at your door; it desires to have you, but you must master it*" (Genesis 4:7b).

Suddenly, the tone of the conversation turned. At first, God showed compassionate observation, then gentle guidance, and now a stern warning. Why the sudden change? No doubt the mood altered because the topic was different. God was no longer talking about Cain; He was talking about the sin that was waiting to overtake him. God hates sin. He never takes it lightly and always approaches it unyielding.

God hates sin because when we refuse to rid it from our lives, more is destined to come. Like a plague of locusts with an insatiable appetite, it launches a precise plan designed to invade, conquer, and demolish every facet of our lives. In the end, its only goal is to leave us barren and desolate, something God never wants for our lives.

As God broaches this topic of sin, He is relentless and to the point. Amazingly enough, however, He is not overly specific. He warns Cain about sin crouching at the door but never mentions what sin. Wouldn't you want to know? I would. What kind of sin was this anyway? Wouldn't it be best for Cain to have a more specific warning, especially now?

Once again, God was not specific because He didn't have to be. Cain knew to what He was referring. Lack of knowledge was not his problem; a desire not to turn from his sin was.

The sin lurking at Cain's door was greed. Jealous that his brother's offering pleased God more, he could have changed what he gave, but he could not manage to bring himself to give God his very best. He wanted God's favor, knew how to get it, but didn't do it. This is why God voiced a stern warning.

We all need a good warning at one time or another. It's part of the reality check that helps get us back on track. We need it as adults, and our children need it as well. Whenever their behavior is erratic or drastic, they need to be approached just as God approached Cain. Note what you see in their behavior, offer godly guidance, then, if necessary, send out a warning of what will happen if they do not turn course. You may be met with opposition, but that is not your concern. Your responsibility is to follow through with these three steps, then leave the fourth step to your child.

STEP #4 – LEAVE THE CHOICE TO THEM

It wasn't long after God spoke with Cain that Abel was dead. With God's final words to master the sin that was about to overtake him still ringing in his ears, he invited Abel out into a field and killed him (Genesis 4:8).

How it must have broken the heart of God to watch as the sin He had warned Cain about so effortlessly overtook him. Even an appointment with God Himself did not change the heart of this angry brother. He heard the truth from the author of truth, and refused to change his mind. Why? How could this happen and what hope do we have when attempting to guide our own children?

It all boils down to free will, the one thing God has given to us all. Just as Cain had a choice, so do our children and all the good and godly counsel in the world can never override what they decide in their heart to do. Cain knew right from wrong but set it in his heart to sin. And even though God could have changed it, He did not because He will never override the free will He has given us.

While this may sound cruel, it is actually the ultimate form of love. Never making us robots forced to do as He commands, God gives us the choice to follow Him and be blessed or not. The mere fact that God spoke directly with Cain, and he still sinned, should give you and me great comfort, for it releases us from the unnecessary burden of feeling responsible for what our children do.

The choice your child decides to make is ultimately his or hers alone. You cannot make your children get along with one another or accept their positions in the family. Hard as you may try, the choice is up to them whether they accept their call in life or not. You cannot force them to do anything they refuse to do; you can only support and guide them in the way they should go.

Perhaps the sibling rivalry in your home has burdened you with guilt, making you feel as though you are a failure as a parent. If so, let me give you some encouragement.

If you determine to respect your child for who he or she is and guide them in the way of the Lord, and they go astray, it is not your fault. Far too often we proudly take credit when our children come out good, then condemn ourselves endlessly when they take a wrong turn. In truth, we have no right to take credit either way. The paths our children take in life, and the attitude they have along the way, are entirely up to them. All we can do is teach, guide, and direct them.

If you are plagued by guilt, give it to God. He understands our role as parents like no one else because He is *our* Father. Ask Him to help you parent each of your children just, as He Himself would, then leave the outcome in His hands. There is no better place to entrust your children.

YOUR ROLE AS PARENT

By profession I'm a nurse, but I have since exchanged my career in medicine to write, teach, and speak to women. As much as I loved being a nurse, I adore encouraging women in the word of God even more. Giving aid to those who are sick and dying brought great pleasure, but caring for those who are hurting spiritually brings even greater satisfaction.

The most important job I will ever have, however, is one I don't get paid a cent to do, be a mother to my children. With no overtime, no vacation time, no health benefits, no employee discounts, and no retirement plan, I am technically their mom for "free." With a payroll that works in reverse, I do all the work and they receive the benefits.

It's a labor of love and I wouldn't change a single thing. With the exception of God and their father, I love my children more than anything else in this world. For this reason I owe them my very best. They deserve my best attitude, finest teaching, undying prayers, and unfailing love.

Some parents, however, believe their children owe them. Like biological servants, they feel as though their child was born to meet our own needs. I don't agree, at least not with this attitude. I believe we as parents have an obligation to give our children our very best because they are not our own. They are on loan from God and must be handled with utmost love, respect, and honor.

Of course this doesn't mean we are to give them everything they want. It simply means we must carefully guide and direct them in the ways of the Lord, which of course takes great effort and time on our part. As a result, parenting is not only a tough job, but also one not to be taken lightly.

The number one thing God wants from parents is to raise godly offspring (Malachi 2:15). For He knows that if we do not, it weakens mankind. As each generation's knowledge of Him is diluted, we drift farther and farther away from Him until eventually sin takes over, stealing souls from His kingdom at a record rate.

Our job is to not allow this to happen, and it starts in the home. We are to know God's word and teach it to our children, so they can teach it to their children. One way of doing this is by praying for your children. I pray for my children in four distinct ways.

YOUR CHILD'S SALVATION

What good it is if a man gains the whole world yet loses his soul? (Mark 8:36) It's a good question to ask not only of ourselves, but also of our children. Why pray for your child's grades, career, or job if he or she does not know Christ as Savior? No amount of success in the world can ever replace eternal salvation, for it is as fleeting as breath (Proverbs 144:4) and has no eternal value.

My husband and I prayed for our children before they were ever conceived, and believe it or not, I pray for my grandchildren who have not been conceived. I pray for God to bless the Douglas name so that it will glorify Him in all we do. I ask God to anoint each consecutive generation in our family line with a passion for Him that is greater than the one before, and I believe wholeheartedly that He is honoring my request.

God wants to seal the heart of every one of your children in His name. He wants to use them for His good work and He will, but you must first pray for their salvation. Don't ever let the enemy tell you your child is too old or too far gone to receive Christ. Nothing is impossible with God.

Before his conversion, the apostle Paul hunted down Christians with the sole intent of having them killed, and he couldn't have been farther from God than the day he walked the road to Damascus. But God had a plan for this man, and once converted, used him to write much of the New Testament. His testimony gives us hope that it is never too late for any child to come to God.

Never entertain the thought that it's too late for your child. Prayer is an extremely powerful tool that is painfully underestimated. Don't undervalue its place in your family. Pray for the souls of your children and do it until your dying breath if that is what it takes. Then trust God to call their hearts to Him.

YOUR CHILD'S HEART

The heart is the wellspring of life (Proverbs 4:23). This means that all we do, and why we do it, originates in our heart. While the mind offers solutions and devises plans, the motive in which it is done is conceived in the heart, and that's what God looks at first and foremost.

I've adopted a personal habit over the years of praying particular characters of the Bible over each family member. For instance, Jimmy has always reminded me of Joseph, the one thrown in the well by his brothers. He reminds me of Joseph in many ways, but most notably by his desire and ability to resist sexual temptation.

As one who travels full-time, the first thing he does when he enters a work place is set the ground rules. He starts by telling the women he works with that he cannot have lunch or dinner with them alone. He then proceeds to tell the guys he does not drink alcohol, gamble, or go to strip bars.

Of course he doesn't announce this the moment he walks in the door, and he does it lovingly, but as these issues come up, which they consistently do, he sticks by his guns.

His ability to remain steadfast and true to God reminds me so much of Joseph that I pray for him to be like him even more. After all, Joseph was one man of the Bible whom nothing negative was ever written about. That's the kind of man I want in my life!

I also pray Bible characters over each of my children. When Drew went off to college I began praying for him to be like Daniel, the one who stood tall and strong in Babylon. Sure enough, each year as I pray for him in this way, his love for God and the conviction to do His will is strengthened more and more.

For Dani, I ask God to protect and provide for her as He did Mephibosheth, the disabled son of David's best friend Jonathan. After Jonathan's death, when David took the throne, Mephibosheth lived as a helpless invalid. Unable to walk, he was left at the mercy of whoever would take care of him.

As an act of compassion to his deceased friend, David asked if there was anyone left in Jonathan's family to whom he could show kindness (2 Samuel 9:1). That's when Mephibosheth was pulled from obscurity, presented to David, and allowed to eat at the king's table every day.

The story of Mephibosheth gives me hope. Hope that God will provide for Dani when her father and I go home to be with the Lord. It gives me a solid hope to grab onto when praying for her because I know if God would provide for Mephibosheth, He will surely provide for our little Dani. This hope gives me great peace.

Then there's myself. I need so much prayer that I ask God to help me be like two people of the Bible: Hannah (Samuel's mother) and Nathanael (one of the twelve disciples).

Like Hannah, I want to be able to offer my children to the Lord. I want to be faithful to the Lord in all my ways and have a willingness to sacrifice that which I love most, for Him. I adore her story of courage and commitment and can't wait to meet her in heaven. There is a park bench reserved for us in the New

Jerusalem, and I look forward to sitting down with her to have a chat once we meet in eternity.

The second person I pray to be like is a disciple, a rather obscure one at that. While I admire them all, there is one disciple with a particular character quality I desire most: a heart with no guile.

"When Jesus saw Nathanael approaching, he said of him, 'Here is a true Israelite, in whom there is nothing false" (John 1:47 NIV). The King James Version describes Nathanael's heart as one with no guile. In other words he was not a crafty, devious, or cunning man. At his very core, Nathanael was honest and Jesus wasted no time making note of it. Before Nathanael even had a chance to shake Jesus' hand hello, the diagnosis of his heart was publicly announced.

Of all the things Jesus could have said to Nathanael, the purity of his heart is what was pointed out. What a compliment and honor to be noted for the goodness that lies deepest within. I want that, and I want it in full. Hearts that are cunning and devious deceive themselves and I don't ever want to be deceived, especially by myself. I want to be known as an honest person by everyone around me, and most of all by God Himself.

Pray for you children's hearts. It is the wellspring of life. Pray that it will overflow with a love for God, and choose a Bible character to guide you in your prayer. Soon you'll be amazed at the similarities you will begin to see in them and the character you pray over them.

YOUR CHILD'S MIND

"The mind is a terrible thing to waste." These are the words of an old public service announcement, and they are so true. The mind is indeed a horrible thing to squander. This is why we should pray not only for our own minds, but also for the minds of our children.

The heart and mind are so closely linked it's sometimes difficult to distinguish between the two. Like rowers in a boat, they work in tandem toward a desired destination. Motives that lie deepest in our heart serve as the rudder, while the mind figures a way to execute the plan.

1 Corinthians 28:9 describes this close link when it says, *"And you, my son Solomon, acknowledge the God of your father, and serve him with wholehearted devotion and with a willing mind, for the LORD searches every heart and understands every motive behind the thoughts. If you seek him, he will be found by you; but if you forsake him, he will reject you forever."*

Once we've prayed for our child's heart, we must next pray for his or her mind, for it is the battlefield of the enemy. Life in the physical world is tough enough as it is, but the combat that poses the most danger occurs in the mind. *"For our struggle is not against flesh and blood, but against the rulers, against the authorities, against the powers of this dark world and against the spiritual forces of evil in the heavenly realms*" (Ephesians 6:12 NIV).

Just as you pray for the cleanliness of your child's heart, pray also for the purity of his or her mind. Idle minds are the devil's workshop, but so are minds that are too busy to think of God. Pick one day from each week and pray for the minds of your children. Ask God to equip them with the ability to detect the schemes of the enemy. Pray they will detest that which is bad and crave only what is good. When you see a flaw in your child, instead of criticizing it, ask God to shore up this weakness then watch as he answers your prayer.

The mind is an invisible battlefield that is very real and vulnerable. Without prayer, our children walk in enemy territory without defense. They need our prayers and we owe it to them. It's is the least we can do.

YOUR CHILD'S PHYSICAL WELL BEING

Do you worry about your children? Just watching the local news is enough to spark fear and worry in the heart of any parent. But no matter how we try to justify our fears, worry is a sin. As a blatant distrust in God, it is never an accepted practice in His eyes.

Jesus wasn't bored or searching for a pithy thing to say when He told His disciples, *"Do not let your hearts be troubled. Trust in God; trust also in me"* (John 14:1). He said exactly what He meant to say and expected them to implement it into their lives. With death only hours away, He spoke words that were pertinent and precise. The disciples needed to hear them then, and we need to hear now.

The word *trust* in this verse means to believe. It involves putting all our faith in God, so much so that worry is no longer an option or desire. When it comes to our children, like Hannah, we must place them in the hands of God and trust He will take care of them. We do our part to ensure their safety but leave their welfare primarily up to Him. When we do this, we do ourselves the great favor of inviting peace into our lives.

When I meet women who are professional worriers, I tell them that worry is nothing but an opportunity to pray. Every time you find yourself looking inward and worrying about all the horrible things that could go wrong, look up into the face of God and give it to Him. This simple but vital change in focus is all it takes to transform useless worry into prevailing prayer. It will change the way you view your child's safety, and bring a sense of tranquility to you and your child.

Whether normal or with special needs, pray for your children. They are precious gifts from God, and like jewels, bring brilliance into our lives. Unfortunately, many are not seen as such and are tossed aside without a second thought. Mistreated, abused, and neglected, they never hear of the great potential that lies within them. What a tragedy when this happens. Don't let it happen in your family. At least once a day, offer a word of encouragement to your children and then pray for them without ceasing. They will begin to grow in ways you never dreamed possible, and you will be amazed.

CHAPTER SEVEN

The Meaning of It All

I could barely contain my tears as I stood before the little lambs. With the storm clouds now lifting and heading off toward the east, streams of sunlight warmed my back as I stood staring at the ground. The freshly cut grass was meticulously trimmed around each and every headstone. The tiny white concrete lambs were no exception.

Guided by vivid memories from my past, I quickly identified them after taking only a few steps into the cemetery. My grandma and grandpa were buried to the right, but I felt drawn to the left. I couldn't recall. Were there four or five little statues?

From a distance it was hard to distinguish. It looked like four, but was there yet another at the very end? The white dot looked vaguely like the others, but if it were indeed another headstone, it was not only the tiniest one of all, but awkwardly close to the fence.

Zig zagging my way through the headstones; I made my way to the figures I remembered seeing as a child. Uncomfortably close to the old rickety graveyard fence, it looked as if there was indeed a fifth lamb at the very edge. It was still difficult to see, so I stooped down for a better look.

At first I thought it was trash, then a tipped vase with a single white flower in it. Inching closer still, it slowly came into focus. Neither trash nor a discarded vase, it was the headstone of a poor mother's fifth beloved child.

No names, dates, or ages marked any of the lambs. No accolades, tributes, or honors boasted of their accomplishments. They hadn't owned businesses, founded organizations, participated in local rotary clubs, or possessed any amount of money. No boyfriends, girlfriends, proms, or marriages. They never had that chance, for they died before, at, or soon after birth. Only a marker, the image of a lamb, speaks in memory of these children who touched the world like a whisper.

What is the meaning of it all? Why did five innocent children have to die so young? How do a mother and father endure such unimaginable pain? What possible worthwhile purpose could there have been for such repeated assaults? Did this marriage survive? Were they able to have other children? Did they grow bitter over their loss, or learn to forgive? What did it do to their relationship with God, and how many times did they too stand atop the same soil staring at their precious lambs and wonder why?

Live just a little and these kinds of questions become a part of life. Left unanswered they can gain enough negative momentum in our lives to make us cynical and doubting of God. Knowing the benefits and the purpose behind pain, however, is a sure way toward greater healing and restoration, which is why we must understand and believe God has a purpose and plan in all He allows into our lives.

GREATER FAITH

"Simon, Simon, Satan has asked to sift you as wheat" (Luke 22:31). Such were the haunting words spoken to Peter by Jesus during the Last Supper. Disturbingly accurate, they became reality only a few hours later, plummeting Peter into a burning pit of despair. Christ saw it coming, predicted the event, and granted Satan's request to sift this man He loved so much.

Scripture is clear, God allows suffering. He sees a particular trial coming our way and permits it into our lives. He knows a child is going to be born with a disability, and He allows it to occur. He warns believers that trials are destined to come our way (1 Thessalonians 3:3); yet, in great wisdom and love does not prevent them from becoming reality.

The million-dollar question is why? Why does God permit suffering that He not only sees coming, but could also prevent? Believe it or not, trials are not a symptom of God's neglect or abandon. They do not expose a dark side of Him that gains pleasure from our pain, and they certainly do not reflect His inability to prevent them from occurring. Nothing could be further from the truth! Tribulations of life are in fact evidence of His love.

Yes, you read correctly. Our struggles are proof that God loves us with an everlasting love, one that seeks to teach, guide, and strengthen all who walk with Him. With great precision, like a scalpel in the hands of a surgeon, hardships work to cleanse and purify the hearts of all who believe in Him (Hebrews 12:5-6). As greater cleansing is achieved, we are then able to draw nearer to Him.

When life gets tough and refuses to let up, there's one thing you never want to lose, and that is hope. Despair to the point of hopelessness is the most frightening feeling in the world. I know because I've been there. Like a tether to sanity, once hope is lost, despair can drive anyone to do anything.

This is why believers, especially parents of children with challenging needs, must understand that all suffering, no matter what kind, serves a grand purpose. One designed for our good and God's glory.

Romans 5:3-4 (NIV) describes this purpose well as it instructs us to, "...*rejoice in our sufferings, because we know that suffering produces perseverance; perseverance, character; and character, hope.*" Notice the three key character traits that lead to hope. Like nothing else, suffering, perseverance, and godly character link us to hope, and in their entirety, these qualities equip us to survive even the most grueling challenges that come our way.

Like a fine-tuned engine, when allowed to run full throttle, pain ignites a fire that produces determination in the heart of a believer. It's what they call chutzpah (hutzpah) or nerve. Far from giving in and going under, tribulations can cultivate greater fortitude and willpower in the one under pressure. As a result, that person does not give up easily and endures remarkably well, glorifying God in the end.

Self-control in the midst of life's greatest trials is something we all want and need. Unfortunately, many buckle under the pressure of distress because they do not understand the purpose behind it. Focusing on the pain and problems at hand, they miss the higher calling and opportunity for greater growth.

Like everything in life, it's our choice whether to persevere through trials or not. Just as no one can force you into greener pastures, no one can keep you out of them either. The choice you make is yours and yours alone, which leads us to the third link that tethers us to hope in the midst of great trials, character.

When Jesus warned Peter that Satan wanted to "sift" him (Luke 22:31), it didn't mean a gentle jostle, it meant an internal trembling. As if predicting a seismic earthquake, Jesus forewarned Peter that he was about to be tested at his very core and like never before. His faith was about to be exposed for what it truly was.

Peter failed miserably. Denying Christ three times, he did what he said he would never do, so he went outside and wept bitterly (Luke 22:62). Sifted, shaken, and suffering, Peter's faith was painfully tested and exposed for what it was: weak and fragile. He didn't pass the test, but God used it for good. Peter's collapse spurred a matchless determination within him. From that moment on, he began to live up to the name originally given to him by Jesus three years before, "Petros" which means *rock*.

As the founder of the first church of Christ, Peter began to preach to surrounding nations and eventually wrote two New Testament letters. Though once fallen, he was now victorious because he allowed his pain and suffering to build him up rather than tear him down.

To glory in our trials is to understand their greater purpose; in turn we receive great hope. In this hope we confidently anticipate all that God has to offer beyond the suffering. With eyes off the temporal and fixed on the One who holds our true reward, we are able to endure much more than we could ever imagine. In the end we are able to reckon it a joy!

GREATER JOY

I'm embarrassed to admit it, but it's only been recently that I've learned to count my trials as a joy. Nineteen years of fussing and fuming with God over what He has allowed into my life, and I am just now beginning to understand what it means to delight in the experience.

Don't get me wrong. I don't enjoy the trials that come my way. They are grueling and often leave me exhausted and depleted. In spite of it all, however, they've recently taken on a different tone in my heart. What used to feel like a painful imposition, now feels more like a divine lesson God is seeking to teach me.

It took me years to figure this out, but as I look back on all the difficult times we've had with our daughter's disabilities, I now see that each trial has served to make me a better person. I couldn't see it at the time, but each challenge burned away a part of me that needed to go. In the end, I came out better than I was before.

Remember Shadrach, Meshach, and Abednego? They were the three friends of Daniel who were thrown in the fiery furnace. Because they would not bow down and worship the golden image of Nebuchadnezzar, the king sought to burn them alive, so he ordered the furnace to be heated seven times hotter than normal. Bound by the strongest soldiers and fully clothed, these men of God were tossed into a fire that was so scorching it killed the men who threw them in.

Committed to God to the very end, they clung to their faith in God even as they were tossed into the oven. For all intents and purposes, the only way out appeared to be through death, but to everyone's astonishment, they did not perish.

"Then King Nebuchadnezzar leaped to his feet in amazement and asked his advisers, "Weren't there three men that we tied up and threw into the fire?" They replied, "Certainly, O king." He said, "Look! I see four men walking around in the fire, unbound and unharmed, and the fourth looks like a son of the gods." (Daniel 3:24-25 NIV)

In the midst of the worst day of their lives, Jesus walked with these faithful men. Not a hair on their head was singed or a thread of their garments scorched. They didn't so much as smell like smoke when they walked out of the inferno (Daniel 3:27). The only things burnt in the flames were the ties that had been fastened around their hands and feet.

Before the fire, they were bound and powerless in the hands of the enemy, but afterwards they walked freely and victoriously with their Lord. Who they were when they went into the fire was not who they were when they came out. They had been changed for the good and it was clear for all to see, even the evil king Nebuchadnezzar.

Such should be our goal when fiery trials come our way. With eyes fixed on God, we triumphantly walk through the fire with Him as the ties that bind us are burned away.

James, Jesus' half brother, tells us to consider it pure joy when we face trials (James 1:2-3), which makes me wonder if

Jesus ever told his little brother this story of Shadrach, Meshach, and Abednego (Christ was the one who had walked with them in the fire you know). Perhaps on a Nazareth hillside, under a dark starry sky, He told small James how these godly men came out of the fire freer and more liberated than when they went in. Maybe He told him this story so that he, too, would believe, teach his children, and eventually instruct us, that trials really do serve a valuable purpose in all of our lives. Rather than barriers or obstacles, tribulations are tools that God uses to tear down and rebuild those who trust in Him. For this reason, we should consider them pure joy!

It's been said that hardships are mere obstacles we should use to climb up onto higher ground. What great wisdom. Just think how many lives would be changed for the better if we'd all adopt this philosophy: instead of following the path of least resistance, choose to trust that God is in control, climb up onto the trial, and move onto higher ground. I don't know about you, but I want this to be my life's motto.

One advantage of getting older is that it gives me a chance to observe trends. One trend I've noticed in my life is that I learn least when things are abundant and most when life is tough. I know beyond a shadow of a doubt that an easy life could have never brought me closer to God like Dani's disabilities have. God knew a calm and peaceful life would not kindle a fire hot enough to burn away the ties that held me captive. Only through life-long suffering and sacrifice could true freedom be found, which is exactly why He allowed Dani to be born the way she is.

God cares more about our character than our comfort. If you are waiting for Him to scoop you up, erase all your problems, and place you back down into a bed of roses, think again. Every trial, irritation, annoyance, and frustration has been allowed into your life to help you become more like Christ. Being thrown into the furnace is frightening and painful, but it's been lovingly designed to help you walk closer with God so that in the end you come out freer than you were went you went in.

I never enjoy pain and I don't think fondly of the challenges that come my way, but I do find joy in what they bring. Knowing they make me more like Christ, I persevere through each trial trusting that it will bring me closer to God. I have found it adds a whole new dimension to my life as it brings immeasurable hope and greater purpose. I pray you learn to do the same with your own adversity.

GREATER AWARENESS OF GOD

Though God is everywhere all the time, I am convinced He makes Himself uniquely available at certain times. It's sort of like the train that runs through our town. Four miles away from our home, I can hear its horn at three o'clock in the morning as it rolls through town, but only when the weather is cool.

Perhaps a meteorologist could better explain the atmospheric details. All I know is that the cool night air of fall and winter transmits the whistle best. Sound asleep under a thick down comforter, I can hear it as it rolls through town in the early hours of the morning, but rarely do I hear it in the summer when only a light blanket is atop me. The conditions have to be just right, and when they are, it's very pleasing to the ear.

Greater awareness of God is much like the whistle of the train. When conditions are right, He will be heard. Given the right temperature, wind direction, and stillness of our soul, we will hear Him when He speaks. We just need to pull our heads out from under the covers and listen to what He has to say.

I wish hearing God was as simple as the sound of the train in the crisp fall air. If it were, I'd set my alarm for three o'clock every morning. The truth is, I often miss His attempts to speak to me as I sleep the night away. Busy doing my own thing, mending my own problems, or fighting with Him on issues I know nothing about, I miss the wisdom He seeks to teach me.

From experience, I can tell you that some of the most life-changing words I've heard from God have been when I was the most desperate. Crying alone in the tub is often where He speaks to my heart. I can't count how many times I have been so exasperated that I've gone into the bathroom, turned on the bath water, and climbed into the tub for a good, hard cry. There is something about this time alone and in distress that always ushers in the presence of God. Of course you don't have to be in the bathtub to hear God speak to you. He will respond to you even if you are in the belly of a whale.

I love the story of Jonah. As one called to bring the word of God to a wicked city, he ran in the opposite direction. With absolutely no love for Nineveh, he refused the call of God only to find himself in a perfect storm, crying out in despair.

Jonah knew what the Lord had called him to do; yet he refused to do it. Choosing to fight God tooth and nail, he ran to the nearest seaport, boarded a ship, hunkered below deck, and went to sleep. When the ship set sail, and the storm reached its peak, all aboard knew it was because Jonah was running from God. He told them so himself. (Jonah 1:10)

In a desperate attempt to save everyone's lives, Jonah instructed the crew to throw him into the sea (I guess he was too scared to take the leap for himself). So they tossed him over the side and the sea grew calm. The Lord provided a great fish to swallow Jonah and there he sat for three days and three nights. Just enough time to sort things out.

Much as I've parked myself in the bathtub and cried out to God, Jonah sat in the belly of the fish and prayed, too. With seaweed wrapped around his head, he had to have been a sorry sight. Once a rebel on the run, he was now a humbled man in the perfect place to hear the voice of God.

After Jonah repented of his sin, God commanded the fish to vomit him onto dry land. Told again go to Nineveh and proclaim the message of God, Jonah did what he was originally called to do. As a result, an entire city turned to God.

Sometimes, like Jonah, we don't want to do what God is calling us to do. Dreading the call, we turn on our heels and run the other direction, only to come head-to-head with greater distress down the line. Troubles, like seaweed wrapped around our heads, take on a life of their own until we find ourselves in a whale of a predicament.

Jonah was called to preach to Nineveh. I, like you, have been called to parent a disabled child. None is what we would have initially chosen to do, but we must determine to accept the call. It isn't necessarily going to be easy, and there will be times when you'll feel frightened and overwhelmed, but God is always at our side. In the end we will be blessed with increased faith, new joy, and a greater awareness of God. Once we've gained these three things, it's time to set our attention on others.

GREATER COMPASSION FOR OTHERS

I boarded the plane with tears in my eyes. My jaws were tight and the corners of my mouth were drawn downward. I was glad to be among the first to board because I looked as though I was buckling under the pressure of flying, but that wasn't the case at all. I was about to cry because of what I had seen just moments before walking down the ramp onto the plane.

Because of Dani and her disabilities, we stood at the gate with tickets in hand, waiting to board early. Alongside us was a woman with her children in strollers and two disabled adults. One was an elderly man with an oxygen tank, the other a man in his thirties with a walker.

My heart went out to the elderly man on oxygen, but for some reason an extra measure went out to the younger man with the walker. As he walked he was very slow and unsteady, making it appear as though even a small snag on the carpet could send him toppling down. His fragility caught my attention and touched my heart. I couldn't help but wonder what it must be like to be so weak and vulnerable.

His approach to the desk was lengthy, so my eyes began to drift around the waiting area. I gave a fleeting look at my daughter who was itching to board the plane, and then around the room at other passengers waiting to board. Seeing nothing particularly interesting, I looked back at the man with the walker to check on his progress.

As my eyes fixed back on his frame, I heard a female voice say, *"Can I walk down the ramp with him to the plane?"* Considerate but firm, the attendant replied, *" No, I'm sorry you cannot."* That's when I saw the helpless woman at the counter. It was his mother.

As a perfect stranger, I saw the frailty of this young man the instant I laid eyes on him. I could only imagine what was running through the mind of his mother. No doubt her concern for his ability to travel alone was grounded in years of experience as his primary caregiver. She'd seen how the littlest thing could become his biggest obstacle, not to mention the countless injuries incurred after attempting a task that was simple and easy for everyone else.

Doctor's visits, stitches, broken bones, and countless other ailments that had become a part of her life the day he was born, weighed heavy on her heart as she watched him attempt to board the plane alone. How would he manage without her there to anticipate his every need? Who would ever care for him as she had so painstakingly done all his life? She had to wonder all these things as she watched this special son leave her side.

I can't know all the things this mother felt as her son boarded the plane, but I do know how I felt as I watched the scene unfold. I rarely cry in public and do whatever I can to prevent it from happening, but their good-bye at the gate broke my heart and reduced me to tears.

To my knowledge, no one else in the waiting area shed a tear over the incident, not even my husband. Everyone boarded as if it was any other day, but I could hardly speak by the time I buckled my seat belt. The scene between this mother and son played over and over in my head. First, I'd hear the mother's appeal, then the rejection, and finally the son's soft words, *"Good-bye Mom"* as he began his long descent toward the plane.

The mother's concerns were valid. He was the first to board the plane, followed by the man on oxygen, then the mother with her children and strollers. By the time we stepped foot on the craft, the woman's son was still working hard to maneuver his way into the seat. He made it, but it was painstakingly slow. I passed him with tears in my eyes, still thinking of his mother standing at the desk.

Why did this scene have such an impact on me? Interestingly enough, air safety could not have been further from my mind. Terrorism? Not a concern. Engine trouble? What are the odds? But the sight of this mother and her son brought me down like a house of cards.

After a little time of prayer, God helped me understand why it touched me so deeply. It's because, though I don't know what it's like to be hijacked or experience significant plane trouble, I do know what it's like to be the mother of a disabled child. Watching this fellow parent as she struggled to release her child out from under her protective wing cut me to the quick, because it is a familiar scenario that has played out in my heart time and again.

You see, if there is anything I understand, it's being the parent of a weak and defenseless child. While all children are vulnerable, those with special needs are even more so and for the rest of their lives. It's a whole new ball game that's very hard to play and never ends.

With nineteen years of adversity tucked under my belt, my heart went out to this mother in a very special way that day. I cried and I prayed for both her and her son, and I think it's safe to say few, if any others did. I don't say this to brag. I say it to emphasize yet another benefit pain and sorrow bring into our lives; the ability to show compassion and offer comfort to others in need.

Unfortunately, I couldn't put my arm around this mother at the airport gate that day. I couldn't even speak to her, but I saw her distress and did what I could do at the time. I simply prayed for them both. First asking God to grant her His peace, then telling Him that I was willing to help the young man if he needed it during the flight. With our seats on opposite ends of the plane, I wasn't sure how this would work out, but I made my offer known to God just the same. It was all I could do.

Isaiah 40:1 (NIV) says, *"Comfort, yes comfort my people!" says the Lord. The best comforters are those who have shared in the same experience."* The Hebrew meaning for "comfort" in this verse means to sigh or breath strongly. It's having pity and compassion for another person in need, and God says those who share in the same experience do it best.

With this in mind, have you ever considered the fact that the difficulties you face in life today could help someone else tomorrow? What good is it if our suffering grows our faith, increases our joy, and bring us into a greater awareness of God, but does not help others?

For me, being able to comfort another parent with a disabled child makes my pain worthwhile. It can't remove the pain in my life, but if I can share what I've learned along the way, I can honestly say it makes it all worthwhile. I can think of nothing worse than persevering through my trials, learning from them, then keeping it all to myself. It cheapens the value of the lesson.

Fellow parent, I challenge you to find the meaning behind your pain. You are not a victim lost and forgotten by God. Quite the opposite! You have been especially chosen for a specific purpose. The situation you are in is one divinely orchestrated to bring about abundant blessings, but first you must trust, believe, and follow God. Running like Jonah will only exacerbate your problems.

Why is your child disabled? How is God involved in your situation? What's the purpose behind the pain? All answers start with a question, so ask God what your heart is seeking to know. No question is too hard for Him, and He won't reprimand you for asking that which you do not know. He will hear and meet you where you are. Go to Him now, ask Him your questions, and then listen for His still small voice. He will speak to you!

CHAPTER EIGHT

Healing

It was a beautiful day. The air was cool as the sun glistened through the orange and red leaves of the trees. The humidity had lifted, there wasn't a hint of rain in the air, and puffy white clouds hung weightlessly in the sky. On the outside, it couldn't have been a more striking day, but on the inside a tempest was brewing deep within my heart.

It had only been three years, but caring for Dani and her disabilities felt as if it had gone on forever. Feelings of anger, frustration and futility were beginning to surface, bringing with them a mighty storm.

I hadn't volunteered to be the mother of a disabled child, I couldn't seem to get used to it, and it was beginning to take its toll on me. Something had to be done, so I did what I had to do; I called a meeting with God. It was time to put all the cards on the table and tell Him exactly what I thought, which is precisely what I did.

I'd just arrived home after taking Dani to school when suddenly, as if out of the blue, I had enough. Talk about being honest with God. This session with Him either earned me a gold medal or knocked a few jewels out of my heavenly crown.

To this day, I don't know what triggered the episode. I only know I was smack dab in the middle of the living room when the storm hit.

It was one of those rare times, spiritually speaking, in which I took off the gloves and got completely honest with God. In the past, I had more or less kept a distance between God and me, labeling it as respect and honor for Him. The problem was, I never got close enough to Him to have a good one-on-one talk. This day, however, was different. I laid it all out: the good, the bad, and the ugly. Every emotion I had kept inside was desperately poured out before Him as never before. Nothing was held back.

I started by telling Him how tired I was with Dani's lack of progress. Then I reminded Him of how many times I had begged Him to heal her, while He remained seemingly distant and uncaring. If that wasn't enough, I went on to point out the fact that our cat gave me more attention than my own daughter, and I was sick and tired of not knowing how to help my own child.

In ten minutes, I had successfully unloaded every grievance that had taken residence in my heart. The storm had hit, and to my amazement, I was still standing. Honesty with God hadn't been so bad after all. In fact, it felt rather good.

Determined to weather it out to the end, I pronounced my closing statement. With tears in my eyes and a bony finger pointing toward the heavens, I shouted my biggest grievance of all… *"Why won't you heal her?"*

I didn't expect a response from Him at all, let alone one that very moment. For years I had wondered why God hadn't healed her, but never heard a response. Today was different, however. Conditions were ideal for me to hear Him speak, and He did.

Calling me by name, He said, *"Nancy, I won't heal her for two reasons. First of all, you want her healed for you. You don't want her healed so much for her sake as you want it for you. You want out. Second, I can do more through not healing her than if I do."*

That was it. God had spoken and His answer was clear. I didn't hear what I wanted to hear, but the truth was remarkably refreshing, so much so I've never again questioned Him on this issue of healing. His words made such an impact on my heart that I continue to ponder them to this very day.

Like a child in need of a good dose of discipline, I had never before considered the fact that my longing for her to be healed was rooted in my own selfish desires. Had any human on earth uttered these words to me I would have pursed my lips, furrowed my brows, and stomped out of the room. But hearing it from God Himself was an entirely different story.

Yes, I loved my daughter very much and wanted only the best for her, but my request had become one that was more for me than for her. God knew it and loved me enough to address it up-front.

The selfishness of focusing on what *I* wanted had inflicted upon me a severe case of tunnel vision. I never considered that God would want anything other than what I wanted; His decision whether to heal her or not was never in question. He was going to heal her; I was convinced.

This notion, however, that God could do *more* through not healing her, now that was a new one. It boggled my mind, prompting me to think outside the box. For the first time in years, I began to realize that God was not only in control, but fully aware of our situation and had a specific plan for our family, one far greater than anything I could ever conceive on my own.

New hope was born again and it did not involve healing.

THE POOL

Can God heal? Without question, He can. God is everywhere, all the time. He is all-powerful; He knows all things, past, present, and future, and loves us more than we'll ever know. He wants the best for all of His children and without a doubt can fully restore anyone, anytime, and anywhere.

Whether God *can* heal a person is not the question. The question to be asked is, will He perform the healing we are asking for.

Going beyond the selfish and superficial, this question takes us straight to the heart of God. In willingness to abandon our own wants and desires, we look beyond what we want and ask God what His will is in a particular situation.

As important as it is to take this question to God, it's a very difficult thing to do, and many never do it. After all, there is always a chance God may say no, and that's the last thing we want to hear when it comes to a loved one who is sick or disabled.

If you think about it, it's easier to ask God for a healing than it is to sincerely inquire His will on the matter. Often times, when we ask God for something this important, we aren't really asking a question that requires a response. Instead, in a very slick and selfish way, we are essentially *telling* Him what to do. It just happens to be in the polite form of a rhetorical question.

It's like when I ask my husband to take out the trash. I am usually not asking him to do it; I'm telling him to. When I say, *"Dear, could you take down the trash?"* I'm actually speaking volumes more. Things like, *"It's your turn - I did it last time. I haven't sat down all day, so you get up and do it. It's overflowing and bugging me to death"* and *"Why do I have to do it all the time?"*

If you don't think you're highly skilled in this covert form of communication as well, think again. Early in life we all learn how to manipulate and control things to get our own way. We do it with our children, our husbands, bosses, co-workers, and worst of all, we do it with God. The problem is, when we attempt to manipulate God, He exposes it for what it really is, which is why we avoid seeking His will on the matter in the first place. Deep down, we know that if we ask our question, then wait for an answer, we may not get what we so desperately want. So, we keep our distance, make demands through polite requests, and then wait for God to do what we want Him to do.

The will of God is a peculiar thing. It's perfect, puzzling, amazing, and mysterious all at the same time. Try as we might, we can never predict it, and even once discovered, it cannot be comprehended in full.

Imagine for a moment how bewildering the Lord's healing must have been for the invalids at the pool of Bethesda (John 5:1-15). Day in and day out, the landscape of the colonnades was saturated with the sick and infirm. Seeking a remote chance for healing, those who were weak and feeble waited for the angel to stir the pool's water.

Only the first person in the water would receive a healing, leaving the rest to wait another week, month, or year. The chance was slim, and no one knew when each stirring would occur. Still they did the only thing they could do; they clung to their last shred of hope.

How discouraging to be anywhere but the water's edge. The farther away from the water they were, the slimmer the odds of healing, and for some, it was virtually impossible. Even those at the pool's edge faced stiff competition. Perched at the rim, they had to maintain vigilant guard, because if they didn't, the opportunity would be lost. Alert every moment of the day, they played a silent game of musical chairs including hundreds of people and only one chair.

Then one day Jesus came. Walking among the colonnades, He maneuvered His way over makeshift crutches and withered limbs as the smell of death, disease, and human waste began to seep into the fiber of His garments. With each step, He gazed into each face in need and perhaps reminisced about the day He formed them in their mother's womb. He yearned for the day these precious children would be whole and complete.

As He made His way through the crowd, one man captured His attention. Hearing he had been disabled for thirty-eight years, Jesus asks him a straightforward question, *"Do you want to get well?"* In a lengthy and roundabout fashion, the man answered, *"Sir, I have no one to help me into the pool when the water is stirred. While I am trying to get in, someone else goes down ahead of me"* (John 5:7). With that, Jesus healed him, he picked up his mat, and walked away.

Broken into simple facts, this encounter appears odd and disconnected. It prompts even more questions about God's sovereign will when it comes to healing. For instance, why did Jesus heal this particular man? Did he hold the record of time spent at the pool? And even if he did, why would Christ heal only one? With so many around Him sick and dying, couldn't He cure at least a few more? And above all, why did Jesus allow His question to go unanswered? Why ask a question and not require an answer?

At first glance, the incident comes across eclectic and disjointed. But with God all things are perfect. He does nothing that is futile or incomplete. He works with great precision that is founded in a flawless plan, and above all, never leaves anyone out.

Though we'll never be able to fathom all the reasons Jesus healed only one person at that pool thousands of years ago, one thing's for sure; physical healing was not His primary concern. Spiritual healing was!

ABOVE ALL THINGS...

Have you ever been used by someone you considered a friend? You thought they liked you for who you were when instead they were using you for their greater gain. Whenever I sense this is happening to me, the first thing to go out the door is my trust for that person. Once trust is gone, I begin to distance myself from them, and if necessary, weed them out of my circle of friends altogether.

There is no faster way to ruin a relationship than for one person to use another for his or her selfish gain. No one wants to be used for what one can give verses who he or she is. It's insulting, offensive, and hurtful.

I personally don't get used a lot by those around me, at least not that I know of. As one who is generally most in need, my friends give selflessly to me, not the other way around. I offer them a lot of prayer and an occasional lunch, but as a rule, I can't give much else. They are gracious friends to me out of the goodness of their hearts, and I love them for it.

But imagine for a moment you are God. All-powerful, all-knowing, and all-present, and you love mankind so much that you never cease calling them to you. You've reached out to them through prophets, priests, and judges, until one day you send your only Son to die for them, so they can spend eternity with you in heaven.

In your final attempt to speak to them, you send them a letter filled with love. Composed over thousands of years and penned only by those who could convey your love best, it was skillfully designed to etch your unfailing love into their hearts.

Unfortunately, your efforts touched only a few. While many say they are your friends, deep in their hearts they only seek to use you for their own profit. With healing, prosperity, and personal gain as their primary goals, their love for you comes second, if at all. They seek your hand and not your face, and it hurts deeply.

No one likes being used and neither does God; He abhors it. Addressing it repeatedly in His word, He firmly instructs us to put Him first in our hearts and minds. No other god is to come before Him, and there are no exceptions. Our holy God and His perfect will are to always remain on the throne of our hearts, for this is how we honor Him.

When Dani was born, I loved God very much. I prayed for her before she was conceived and couldn't wait to receive the blessing I was sure God had just for us.

With the knowledge that disabilities and birth defects were always a possibility, I prepared myself to receive her with open arms, even if she weren't normal. I said I could handle anything, but deep down there was no challenge to this statement. I expected what I had in essence ordered from God, a normal healthy child. Assuming she'd fit perfectly into the family, I waited for my "order" to arrive; sure it was going to be exactly what I wanted.

Soon after her disabilities became apparent, however, this attitude began to change. Suddenly God and I were on opposing sides. Like a bait and switch routine, I felt robbed when I didn't get what I wanted. Presuming God would do as I planned, I was shocked when He refused. As a result, a chasm between Him and I began to develop. I continued to acknowledge Him as my God, but harbored a grudge.

Sensing the void between us, I eventually began making my way back to Him. Still determined to get what I so deeply desired, I began to bridge the gap, but only to engage Him in a wrestling match. Prepared to wear Him down if it was the last thing I would ever do, I planned to nag Him until He caved in.

But no matter what I did, God remained unyielding. Each time I asked for a healing, He would refuse. I'd go to my corner, concoct a new way to ask the same thing, and then return to Him to repeat my request. It didn't matter how passionate or creative I got; His response would always be the same.

Sadly, with each failed attempt, my heart grew more angry and rebellious. Convinced I knew what was best, I stood firm in my request and refused to budge. As a result, our wrestling match went on for many years.

Cloaked in motherly love, my insistence for a healing was really a sin. Refusing to submit to His will, I clung to my own selfish desires, convincing myself healing was the only option. Skillful but ignorant, I repeatedly broke God's first commandment; *"Thou shall have no other gods before Me"* (Exodus 20:3).

I wasn't aware of it then, but each time I refused to accept that which God had purposed for my life, I was in fact rejecting His will. Placing my desires before His, I not only dishonored my daughter for who He created her to be, but also held contempt for Him. Selfish, ungrateful, and unbelieving, sin held me a hostage and far away from true freedom.

I hadn't yet learned the promises of Deuteronomy 28, which guarantee great blessings to those who obey God and keep His commands. From the land we live on to the food we eat, abundant blessings are ours when we place God and His will above our own.

A long list of blessings is included in Deuteronomy for those who honor God's commands, but this one comforts me the most, *"The fruit of your womb will be blessed"* (Deuteronomy 28:4a).

Never lost, forgotten, or abandoned, God promises to bless the children of those who keep His commands. Normal or challenged, every one of our little lambs is safe and accounted for in His loving hands. He will protect them and guide them in all they do and nothing will ever change this, because this is His promise.

When was the last time you thought of God's first commandment? When was the last time you broke it? Perhaps your desire for Him to heal your child is so strong you're past the point of caring what He wants. Maybe you are angry over your child's condition and don't want much to do with Him anymore. Could it be you no longer trust Him as you once did, because deep down you feel cheated?

As parents of disabled children, it isn't unusual to be confused or angry with God. His will is nearly impossible to understand under normal conditions, let alone those as trying as ours. But if you become aware of anything at all, understand that closeness with God must never hinge on our ability to understand His will. An intimate walk with God can only be obtained when our faith in Him is firm and unyielding in all circumstances, especially those we do not understand.

Think back for a moment when Jesus walked among the infirm at the pool of Bethesda. It appeared that only one man was healed while the multitudes were left unchanged. In truth, however, everyone in the vicinity was changed that day.

Since God cares about every person, you can be sure He left no soul untouched that day. Every heart and mind that saw or heard what Jesus did, was tested to the core.

The lame man of thirty-eight years received a healing, then walked away never knowing the One who restored him. He simply picked up his mat and walked away. It took the Jews and their skeptical questions for him to discover he hadn't a clue who healed him. Only when Jesus approached him again at the temple did he discover the identity of his healer. What he did with this knowledge we do not know, but unlike anyone else that day, his heart and body were touched in a very unique way.

The sick and infirm that watched this scene transpire were met with a challenge as well. They were confronted with the choice of seeing their Savior for who He was or keeping their eyes on their infirmity. It was a decision they each had to make.

Only one man got what he wanted that day, leaving them to ponder many things. Would they believe in God who healed another but not themselves? Would they engage Him in a battle and demand a healing, or reject Him altogether? Each heart was left on its own to decide.

Then there were the Jews. Abruptly confronted with their biggest challenge in history, they had to choose whether to acknowledge Jesus as their long-awaited Messiah or turn their hearts the other way. Would they accept Him for whom He was, or honor their man-made religious rules instead? It was a trying day for each and every one of them.

Each person, sick or well, faced a soul-searching decision that day. Christ had walked among them, granting only one a physical healing. Who would follow Him in faith and who would cling to his selfish desires? Only Christ knows who did what, but one thing is for sure, every heart was either hardened or softened by His presence that day.

The same is true for you and me. In all our infirmities, Jesus is present in the hearts of all who believe in Him. Some He chooses to heal, others He does not. Some children are restored and released from their illness, while others are left at the side of the pool, seemingly unchanged.

But, believe it or not, physical healing is not God's primary concern. Spiritual healing is! Whether we get what we want or not, our love for Him must always remain the same. True faith does not demand of God, it humbly asks, waits, and accepts that which He sees fit to give, continuing to love Him through it all.

Years ago, a close family member told us that our daughter was born with disabilities because we lacked faith in God. He believed that had we had enough faith, she would have been born perfectly normal. A bit shocked at the accusation at first, we soon discarded it as rubbish. It simply wasn't true. Faith does not prevent adversity from coming our way; it does, however, determine how we handle it.

While lack of faith is not the issue when it comes to our children being born with a disability, it is an issue when it comes to accepting God's sovereign will in the matter. Jimmy and I have never been able to explain fully why Dani was born the way she is, but we do know beyond a shadow of a doubt, it is part of God's eternal plan. He's allowed this into our lives in order to mold us into the image of Christ. Our job is to accept His will and reflect Him in all we say and do.

What a privilege it is to know that God has not healed our daughter so that He could do *more* through our lives! It goes against all logic, but it's proven to be true, He has done abundantly more through the pain and trials of our lives than if things would have been normal. Caring more for our character than our comfort, God has refined us in a very special and unique way through the pain.

It's taken many years, but now I thank God for our infirmity. Of course I do not wish any child to be sick or disabled, especially our sweet little girl. It's just that I've finally grown to the point where my own desires are second to God's. For the first time in my life, I seek His will and accept my suffering, knowing He has a plan and it is good. Leaving nothing amiss, I've witnessed first hand that God can heal a heart, even if He does not heal the body.

Do you truly seek the will of God, or are you hunting for a way to change His will to match your own? I lovingly warn you never to let your love for your child override the will of God. It isn't worth it. We think we know what is best, but in truth we do not. Take it from King Solomon, the wisest man who ever lived,

"Fear God and keep his commandments,

for this is the whole duty of man"

(Ecclesiastes 12:13b)

What is our purpose in life? According to Solomon, it is our *whole* duty to fear God and keep His commands. It isn't part of our responsibility, or something we do when we feel like it; it's our whole purpose in life.

Before our spouse, children, career, or hobbies, God's will and His commandments are to be first in our hearts and lives. Nothing we desire, not even something as good as the healing of our child, should ever come before Him.

Can God heal? Yes! Is it His will to heal? That is for Him to decide and for us to humbly accept. With wisdom that surpasses any of our own, He deserves our utmost faith and trust, even in heartfelt matters we do not understand.

Give God the honor He deserves. Close any gap you have allowed to come between you and Him, and make amends. Decide to trust Him in all areas of your life, and you will receive true and lasting healing!

CHAPTER NINE

Fear Versus Faith

"I cannot believe this is my life!" These were the words I shouted as I bolted out the door of my mother's home. Things were not going well at the time and the strain of disabilities were testing me to the limit. Seeing the frustration build, my mother offered to take Dani for the afternoon, and it was a good thing because I was ready to explode.

The gesture was kind, and the only thing my mother could do to help, but it wasn't enough. Unable to find joy in the thought of having only a few hours away, I found myself dreading the moment I'd have to pick my daughter up again. A few hours alone simply weren't enough. If I could have had anything in the world at that moment (that was guilt-free and legal) it would have been to drive off into the horizon and never come back. But this was not an option, so I took what was offered, scanty as it seemed.

Like talons in my back, fear was getting a grip on me. Life with disabilities had hijacked our family and was taking it in a whole new direction, one I didn't like at all. We hadn't chosen this path, we couldn't alter the course, and I was convinced we were headed for nothing but disaster.

Still young in my acceptance of the will of God, I had not yet learned to trust Him in every area of my life. I certainly didn't trust Him with things I did not understand, especially those so painful and personal. As a result, fear of the future was quickly becoming a stronghold in my life.

FEAR GRIPS

There are two kinds of fear: godly and ungodly. Godly fear is a respectful awe for God, who He is, and what He stands for. It seeks to know and follow Him wherever He leads, and it does so with utmost reverence. It is the kind of fear God commands us to have (Ecclesiastes 12:13, Revelations 14:7) and is designed to bring us many blessings, one of which is great freedom.

Ungodly fear, on the other hand, is a tool of Satan. With one purpose in mind, its intent is to do whatever it takes to get our eyes off God. It's the more common of the two fears, and one you probably know all too well. With a grip that seeks to suffocate its prey, fear takes hold of you and does not easily release.

Exhibiting itself in every imaginable form, ungodly fear typically manifests itself through worry, panic, paranoia, and dread. With a multitude of medications, therapies, and treatments designed to treat these particular illnesses, ungodly fear is not only a common ailment in our society, but a lucrative one as well.

Aggressive and dangerous, ungodly fear seeks to inhabit anyone who has not made overt plans to keep it out. Even well-meaning Christians can fall victim to its grip, only to find themselves in a miserable prison on a daily basis.

I know from experience how this fear can get its tentacles into our lives and begin to take control. When Dani was born, the prospect of living the rest of my life with a disabled child was so frightful, it began to overwhelm me. One fear would lead to another, which was always bigger and more terrifying. Soon my fear of the future became like a wall before me that seemed impossible to scale, making me feel as though life had ground to a halt.

What was life with Dani going to be like in the future? Will we ever be able to retire? Who is going to take care of her when we die, and how can we be sure she'll be safe and secure once we are gone?

Every possible fear there was came pounding at my door in the form of one question or another. Like brash intruders, they would push their way into my thoughts, striking within me great fear and dread of the future. Panic was never far away and nearly anything could trigger an episode.

Fear paid a particularly memorable visit one day. Hearing its voice clearly, I can still recite the words today. Its goal was to discourage and frustrate, but instead it prompted something entirely different. What the enemy intended for bad, God purposed for good, and when all was said and done I walked away having learned a very valuable lesson.

I had just put Dani in the tub to give her a bath. At twelve years, she filled the tub from end to end. Her increased height made washing her hair and bathing her body the biggest challenge ever, and by the time I got to shaving her legs, my back was burning from the strain.

Kneeling over the tub's edge, I reached for the shaving cream with one hand and lifted one of her legs with the other. After an ample lathering, I commenced shaving. Running the razor up and down her lily-white limb, I began to wonder how in the world I was going to be able to do this when I got older.

In cadence with the razor I began to talk to God asking Him, *"If my back hurts this bad now at forty, how in the world am I going to do this when I am Fifty? Sixty? Seventy? Eighty? Ninety?"* I got up to ninety years old when God intervened by citing His own scripture. He said, *"Just do what you need to do today and don't worry about tomorrow"* referring to Matthew 6:34.

Though my back continued to burn, my question did not. The fiery darts of the enemy, designed to spur on another episode of fear for the future, were effectively extinguished by the soothing word of God.

In relatively few words, God neutralized all the enemy had set out to do, sparing me great heartache and grief in the process. The pain in my back was nothing compared to what the enemy had in store for me that day. Meant to degrade and discourage, Satan's question was nothing less than a spark aimed for my destruction. Sure that I would keep the question to myself and brew over it for hours, days, or even months, he was confident I was in for a good worry. But God had other plans. He not only put an end to a potentially huge fear, but also taught me a wonderful lesson.

I still have to shave her long gangly legs, but now I do so in peace. How I'll care for her over the next ten, twenty, or thirty years I still don't know, because God never explained that part to me. All I know for certain is that He will take care of it, and I have nothing to worry about.

The enemy was slick as he approached me that day by the tub. Knowing the pain in my back was just the thing to prompt me to fear the future again, he was eager to point it out. With hopes it would turn my heart from God, he seized the opportunity with great joy, only this time it did not work.

The extent of our enemy's evil is difficult to comprehend, but it is a very real part of life nonetheless. Satan seeks to devour me, and he is out to destroy you as well. Watching your every move, and noting each response, he works diligently to attack you at your weakest point. Whatever you worry and fret over, that is where you are most weak. Skillfully improving his aim with each assault, he hits you right where he knows it will hurt most.

What venomous words does the enemy spit in your ear? Which areas of your life are nearly breaking your backs producing great fears? If fear, worry, anxiety, panic, and dread are a part of your life, confess them to God. Give them to Him so He can quench your burning pain. He wants to do this for you more than you will ever know. You need only go to Him.

Remember, God is a god of peace; never fear. When we are full of fear and doubt, it is a sure sign we've drifted from Him and are in enemy territory. Earthly problems will never go away, but God is always with us and He seeks to provide our every need. Always aware of the lies we hear, He waits to speak His truth to our hearts, and when He does it's a cooling relief!

I've never again asked God how I will shave Dani's legs when I am old. Instead, each time I lift the razor, I smile as I remember the time God squeezed into my tiny little bathroom, knelt beside me at the tub, and spoke His healing scripture into my heart. I think of how His Son Jesus washed the feet of His disciples, and consider the blessing of doing the same for my little girl. No longer a burden or a fear, it is a pleasure to serve her in this way.

FAITH WHISTLES

I can't recall where we were at the time, but when I was a little girl my mother and I were shopping when we heard a little boy whistling. I didn't think much of it until my mother pointed out an astonishing truth about humans and whistling. She said, *"You know someone is happy when they whistle, because you just can't whistle when you're angry or upset."*

Her philosophy has stuck with me all these years because it's true. You can't whistle in distress. I never whistled during childbirth, and I don't whistle while doing the monthly bills. Whenever I do hear a whistle, however, I know without doubt happiness is near.

The same is true with faith. Much like the happy tune of that little boy long ago, it changes our hearts for the better. Like a whistle, faith is contagious as it prompts us to lift our chin a little higher and see beyond the problems at hand. Even a small brush with faith can bring a smile to our face and a greater measure of joy into our hearts. Whistling peace, assurance, hope, and joy into our hearts, it encourages us to endure many things we never thought we could. In the end we are able to persevere through the greatest of trials, and come out better than before. It's a wonderful thing!

Faith Whistles Peace - *"May the God of hope fill you with all joy and peace as you trust in him, so that you may overflow with hope by the power of the Holy Spirit."* Romans 15:13

How would your describe your heart? Is it full of peace or overflowing with anxiety and stress? With so many things to worry about in the world, it's easy to allow our hearts to drift from peace. As parents with special challenges, a life of pressure is often accepted as normal.

But God is the God of peace. It is never His will for us to be weighed down with the worries of the world. He wants to carry all our concerns on His shoulders, so we can rest in His strong and capable arms. As we seek Him with all of our heart, His presence will more fully reside in us and grant us a peace that passes all understanding. Oh how I want this in my life and yours as well.

Proverbs 14:30 says, *"A heart at <u>peace</u> gives life to the body, but envy rots the bones."* The King James Bible says it this way, *"A <u>sound</u> heart is the life of the flesh: but envy the rottenness of the bones."* In essence, peace of heart brings health not only to our hearts, but ultimately to our body as well. Peace is a healing medicine that restores our body and soul.

Ulcers, high blood pressure, headaches, anxiety, sleeplessness, anger, depression, apathy… all are signs of a heart devoured with worry and stress. Does this describe your heart? I'm not asking if it describes what you project to others. I mean does it describe how you feel deep inside when no one else is around?

Faith in God is balm for our hearts. It brings quietness to the soul like nothing else can, and because God is the great Physician, only He can prescribe the peace we need.

When the enemy whispers a distressing call in your ear, and it prompts you to worry, call on your faith to whistle peace.

Faith Whistles Assurance – *"So this is what the Sovereign LORD says: "See, I lay a stone in Zion, a tested stone, a precious cornerstone for a sure foundation; the one who trusts will never be dismayed. "* Isaiah 28:16

There is nothing like the strength and stability of a father. He is the home's leader, provider, and protector, and if missing, leaves a void no human can fill.

My husband Jimmy has been traveling full-time for nearly eight years. He does it so I can stay home with Dani, and I've learned to live without him four days out of the week, but I'm always ready for him to come home.

Logistically I run the home, but he is the president. We communicate by phone and instant messenger many times throughout the day, which eases the burden immensely. It gives me guidance and keeps him apprised of what's going on here at home. Modern technology is simply wonderful and I love it, but it can never take the place of the presence of my husband. I would never want to do without him.

Jimmy's leadership is the cornerstone of our family. Tried and tested for 24 years, he's proven to be a strong and wise leader of our home. He lovingly accepts his role, which enables me to trust and follow him completely. As a result, I feel safe and secure, even when we are not together. His stability and strength bring assurance and peace like nothing else can, which is a rare commodity in this day and age.

If you are a father, you are the cornerstone of your family. Everyone looks to you for guidance and seeks to follow your lead, but you are only as stable as your foundation. Who is your cornerstone? As a husband and father, you are the leader of your home, but your guidance must come from Christ, who is the head of all homes.

He is the key to your foundation and the only One who can keep you stable and strong in the midst of life's stresses and strains. Only through Jesus can you find strength to walk your family through life without being consumed in the process. Never walk a day without Him guiding your way, for if you do you will surely fall.

Perhaps, however, you are a single mother. If so, I have but a glimpse into your life, and what I see I do not envy. You cannot call or send an instant message to your spouse in order to receive the guidance you need, and everything is on your shoulders.

Whether it's the cleaning, cooking, shopping, discipline, errands, finances, or childcare, it's all on your back, and it's a heavy load to carry.

My heart goes out to you, dear sister, if on top of it all you are caring for a child with special needs. Juggling the responsibilities of a home is extremely difficult in and of itself, but to have disability in the home as well is overwhelming just to think about.

But never be discouraged, dear one, because you, too, have a cornerstone! His name is God the Father. He is the Daddy for your children, Protector for your home, and Companion for your heart. He is the foundation for everyone in your family and He promised to provide your every need. What more secure footing could you ask for?

Unlike a human father, God is never out of town, in a meeting, or out of cell phone range. He never misses a call, does not sleep, and certainly never slumbers. He will never abandon you, is always ready for you to come to Him, and wants to help you with all your needs, no matter how small they may be. Nothing would please Him more than to be the leader of your home, all you have to do is hand it over to Him.

Regardless of what your family dynamics may be, God is able to give you the assurance needed to obtain true and lasting peace. Never let the enemy steal the confidence of knowing that God is your rock and sure foundation. He is now, and forever will be!

When the enemy whispers doubt in your ear, causing you to feel uncertain, call on your faith to whistle the assurance that God is your cornerstone.

Faith Whistles Hope – *"Through whom we have gained access by faith into this grace in which we now stand. And we rejoice in the hope of the glory of God."* Romans 5:2

If there is one shred of hope, I know I can survive. Just one bit of "can do" spirit is all I need. If I have this, I can work my way through any trial, no matter how long, how deep, or how wide it may be.

You know it well by now, and I don't have to remind you: life with disabilities is as long, deep, and wide as it can get. It isn't a road for the weak or faint of heart, and without hope, there isn't a living soul who stands a fighting chance. It's simply too tough to go it alone. We need hope in order to survive.

If there's one movie I love it's *Rocky,* starring Sylvester Stallone. It burst onto the scene over thirty years ago and is still considered one of the greatest movies of all time.

Why do we love *Rocky* so much? What made this poor, dirty, unheard-of boxer so appealing? What did he have to offer that we haven't been offered in countless movies before?

Rocky is a classic because it touches the heart of all who see it. Known as the underdog of underdogs, Rocky Balboa never gave up. Broken, unknown, uneducated, and virtually all alone, he had one crucial thing going for him, the only thing he needed to fight and win... hope.

If you took a happy, healthy, normal little boy and told him he was worthless, useless, and would never amount to anything, he'd eventually believe it. His sense of self value would begin to drop, he'd eventually quit striving to accomplish that which his heart desired most, and given enough time, he'd lose hope all together and self-destruct one way or another.

On the other hand, if you took a child and told him how precious he was and that God had given him very special gifts and talents, he'd likely believe it and strive to do great things. His dreams and goals would be nurtured, and his confidence to achieve them would grow as well. Odds are, at the end of his life, he'd end up doing abundantly more than if he had never heard an encouraging word.

Like glue, hope is the bond that holds us together. Binding us firmly in place, it gives us strength to make it through the day, no matter what that day may bring. And, though it can never keep all of our troubles at bay, it is sufficient to shore us up enough to weather the storms that life will inevitably blow our way.

Like a beacon of light on a distant shore, hope gives us something on which to focus our eyes. As a point of reference that never wavers or shifts, it gives us the stability we need to make it through the most difficult of times.

I don't know about you, but I need the hope of Christ in my life. Each morning before I face the day, I meet with God and ask Him to fill me with His Spirit, the Spirit that brings forth love, joy, peace, patience, kindness, goodness, faithfulness, gentleness, and self-control. Like you, I never know what the next 24 hours will bring, so I grab onto Jesus, my anchor of hope, so I will not stray from His will and fall flat on my face.

Like Rocky Balboa, each day is a challenge. Sure to test my strength and resolve, it is full of training exercises that require me to have ready feet and a focused heart. Keeping my eyes fixed solely on God, I go about each day as if I were training for a big event, because the fact of the matter is, I am.

Most days don't feel like the main event though. They don't involve getting into the boxing ring dressed in my finest boxing shorts. I don't get to stand in front of a crowd and hear them cheer me on, and I certainly don't end the day with a tangible prize. The average day is actually a bit tedious and often quite boring.

I wake up each morning as early as I can, before Dani wakes up, in order to have my time alone with God. It begins in my nightgown then progresses to sweats. More often than not it's just Dani and me together doing our daily routines. I manage the home and she watches her favorite DVD's. We run to the store, eat dinner, cuddle on the couch, and then go off to bed, ending a day that seems like all the rest.

But I've learned that not all days are the same. Each day is a building block that serves to either hold up or weaken the next. A day jump-started with hope renewed in God is like a good day at the gym training for an upcoming match. It gives us just enough strength and power to face the next day and increases our chance of ultimate victory exponentially.

But a day not grounded in the hope of Christ is like setting our feet on shifting sand. Even the smallest of waves can work to weaken and erode our stability until, before we know it, we find ourselves fretting and worrying about even the tiniest of things. Insecurity, fear, and turmoil slowly begin to creep into our lives until triumph is not only a thing of the past, but a long lost dream as well.

But hope is God's way of encouraging us. Telling us to never give up, no matter the odds, He cheers us on like the crowds cheered Rocky on the streets of Philadelphia. *"Give a little more! You can do it! Don't give up!"* and *"I love you!"* are just a few ways He seeks to sustain our hope. He does this because He knows that as the most vital element in our foundation, hope is what we need to survive.

Encouragement is like TNT. All it takes is just one word of support to turn a life around. Of all the people who Rocky knew, only one person believed in him and never left his side. It wasn't his mother and it wasn't his father. It wasn't a brother, neighbor, best friend, boss, or even his trainer. It was one quiet, homely woman who would one day become his wife: Adrienne. Just one little voice of hope and encouragement; that was all he got and that was all he needed. It is all you and I will ever need as well.

Life is full of nay-sayers who love to make it their goal to dash any optimism in sight. Ranking high above them all, Satan is always the first in line to dampen our spirit. Telling us how terrible our lives are and that we'll never get out of our miry pit, his number one goal is to dishearten us to the point where we lose hope, give up, and drown.

But hopelessness need never be our state of mind. God has a perfect and holy plan for every member of your family. He is at your side speaking words of hope, encouraging you to believe in Him. He is asking you to cling to Him and trust that your future is one full of great blessings, many of which are just around the corner.

When the enemy whispers discouraging words in your ear and tempts you to give up, call on your faith to whistle hope.

Faith Whistles Joy – *"Though you have not seen Him, you love Him; and even though you do not see Him now, you believe in Him and are filled with an inexpressible and glorious* joy." 1 Peter 1:8

It always makes us smile to see her special walk. She only walks this way when she is most happy, and as a result it brings great joy to our hearts.

When Dani is in her prime and feeling her best, she walks with one straight leg, the left one to be exact. It can happen anywhere and at anytime, but when she feels delight, she locks that left knee and walks like a pirate.

Jimmy and I have never figured out why she does this, but through the years we've grown to love it. We enjoy it so much we call her "Peg" when she does it. Whichever one of us sees her do it first usually says to the other, *"Peg's with us today!"* Then we all cheer the fact that Peg has graced us with her presence.

Why do we love Peg so much? Because she's fun! Dani always has a good day when Peg pays her a visit. As a result, we reap the benefit as well. We love Peg as if she were our own and would gladly have her reside in our home full-time. She's an absolute delight!

No one likes a grouch or a sourpuss. People that gripe, complain, gossip, and moan are miserable company. Like a black cloud looming over our head, conversation with them leaves us dreading the inevitable downpour of doom and gloom. Unless you are just like them and thrive on negative conversation, instinct prompts you to flee for cover and get as far away from them as possible.

A person full of joy, on the other hand, is an entirely different story. Like faith, they are attractive, enticing, and addicting to those with whom they have contact. Of all the people I've ever known in my lifetime, there are only two people who literally light up a room when they walk in it. Like Santa Claus with a bursting sack of gifts hoisted over his shoulder, their presence exudes a special happiness, which naturally attracts everyone. Their joy is unique, and I wish I could name more than two people who exude this quality. I wish I could name myself, but I can't even do that.

As rare as this commodity may be, joy is something God intends for all His children. Founded in the knowledge of Him, joy blesses everyone in its vicinity with the assurance that God is in control and there is really never anything to worry about.

"Therefore do not worry about tomorrow, for tomorrow will worry about itself. Each day has enough trouble of its own."
(Matthew 6:34)

If it's the last thing you ever do, hang onto your faith and never let it go. It's the most powerful weapon we have to subdue the enemy and it's our only means for survival.

Trust in the One who holds your future in His hand, and then sing a song of courage as you walk the road ahead. Before you know it, your heart will begin to smile, your steps will become lighter, and the burdens of life will begin to fade. Trials and tribulations will still come your way, but faith will keep you grounded and secure in the storm.

When the enemy spits lies in your ear and fear begins to grip your soul, call on your faith to whistle peace, assurance, hope, and joy. No matter what lies ahead of you today or in the future, God will never abandon you or lead you into disaster. Life is never out of control when He is at the helm. It's never His goal to bind, restrict, or confine you. His only desire is to bring you peace and set you free. What a precious Father we have in Him!

CHAPTER TEN

Our Heavenly Reunion

When you think of heaven, what comes to mind? Fluffy clouds? Angel wings? Aimless floating? I can't fully envision this place God is preparing for us, but I tend to think of it as a place full of noes. No bugs, no humidity, no weight gain, no accidents, no crying, no mistakes, no bills, no weariness, no illness, no suffering, no dying, and no cooking; a multitude of long-awaited heavenly noes.

The older I get, the more I look forward to joining God in paradise. When I was in my teens and twenties, however, the thought of going to heaven didn't sound very good at all. I wanted a reservation there, but wasn't ready to go just yet. I had far too many things to do on earth first. I wanted to learn to drive a car, finish college, get married, buy a home, experience childbirth, raise my children, and have grandchildren. I had so much I wanted to do on earth that going to heaven was the last thing on my mind.

God has been gracious to me. With the exception of grandchildren, I've experienced all these things and a whole lot more. I'm more ready than ever to go home and be with the Lord, but I still don't want to go just yet, but not for the same reasons I had as a youth. I want to stay on earth a little longer for two reasons: to care for Dani and to accomplish as much as I can for God.

You don't know this, but I wasted the first half of my life experiencing what the world had to offer. I did all the things I wanted to do, and not a single bit of it was for God. I wandered from Him much like a prodigal daughter, only to discover it wasn't all it was cracked up to be.

Empty and desperate, I returned to God eight years ago and committed the rest of my days to Him and His work. I am now a full-time student in His college of knowledge. I cling to the promise of Joel 2:25, which pledges to repay what the locusts have eaten. With a women's ministry up and running, two books under my belt, and two more in the wings, I do believe the locusts are finally gone and a fruitful crop is in bloom.

Over the past eight years I've seen first hand that God does indeed restore. The most wonderful thing is He does it so fully. It starts here on earth when we give our lives to Him and culminates in a great crescendo when we get to heaven. No more pain, no more suffering and no more grinding fatigue. All things in heaven will be as God originally planned, and it will be nothing short of wonderful!

HEAVENLY RESTORATION

After Christ, the first person I most want to meet when I get to heaven is our daughter Dani. Of all the people on earth, she is the one person I've had the closest contact with, but know least. A mystery to everyone she meets, she still eludes even her father and me.

Though almost completely hidden behind a wall of Autism, Dani is a very sweet, kind, and fun person. She has the patience of Job and the innocent spirit of a child. She wouldn't hurt a fly, never meets a stranger, and has not one ounce of prejudice in her body. Everyone is considered a friend and they all get the same treatment, a warm handshake and a big smile!

I long for the day when we are able to meet and talk fluently with our little girl. How did I do as a mother? What was she trying to say all those times her behavior left me so puzzled? Has she forgiven me for all the times I got angry at her Autism, but took it out on her? Does she know it was never her that frustrated me so, but the disability I despised so much?

Autism has effectively stolen our daughter from us. If you've never met or lived with an individual who cannot communicate, it's difficult to image how much it steals from one's life. Even the littlest thing can be impossible or even dangerous.

When our daughter is hungry, she rarely tells us. I have to know when she last ate, know how much she consumed, and then guess when she might need to eat again. She can't tell us when she is cold, she doesn't sense danger, and is unable to communicate her feelings. Her father and I run on instinct when it comes to meeting her needs. I keep a detailed record of her health conditions, much like I did with my patients at the hospital, and use it to predict the future. She keeps us both on our toes as we work hard together to make her life the best it can possibly be.

Dealing with Autism and all that it steals from an individual is sad, frustrating, maddening, and exasperating, sometimes all at the same time. But life is too short to spend it crying all the time. Sometimes you just have to laugh. Laughter is good medicine, and I've learned to take a hearty dose of it as often as I can, which is precisely what I did one Sunday afternoon after church.

It was a beautiful summer Sunday morning. We were sitting in church, the preacher was preaching a great sermon, and I was taking notes. Glancing down at my note sheet I saw out of the corner of my eye Dani's bra strap had slid off her shoulder. Since I've cared for her for 19 years, she's virtually an extension of myself, so I reached over and put the strap back onto her shoulder.

I went back to listening to the pastor and taking notes when again, I saw her strap fall. Puzzled as to how it could slip again when she hadn't moved a muscle, I promptly placed it back onto her shoulder.

A few minutes later, it was the same song third verse, only this time I poked my index finger and thumb into the armhole of her dress and began fishing around. Finding the plastic piece that tightens the strap, I slid the gadget up toward her shoulder, sure that I had fixed the problem. There was no way that strap could fall again.

But, against the odds, and in spite of several fishing trips, that crazy strap continued to fall time and time again. Each time it would drop, I'd shorten it a little more, but no matter what I did the silly thing refused to stay up.

I couldn't understand what I was doing wrong. I've worn bras for thirty-seven years and never encountered a never-ending strap before. All I could think to myself was, *"How short does this strap have to get before it can't fall anymore?"* Bound and determined to win, I fought that strap the entire service.

It wasn't until we got home, as I was helping her change out of her dress, that I saw what I had really been doing to her while the pastor preached. To my utter amazement, I had tightened her bra so tight that the bottom edge of it was hiked up above her breasts and had become a turtleneck of sorts! My poor child, whom I thought I kept well groomed, had walked through church and attended Sunday school with a noose-like bra around her neck, and it was all my doing.

Staring at the sight I nearly laughed my head off when I saw what I had done. We all had a good laugh that day after church, but deep down in my heart it hurt to know that my little girl couldn't tell me what I was really doing to her during the church service.

The incident itself was harmless, but it would have never occurred if she had the ability to communicate normally. It's always been painful for her father and me to not know what she's thinking or how she feels. Can you imagine what it would be like to have an opinion and never be able to express it? How dehumanizing it would be, yet that is the world in which our daughter lives. Perhaps it's the world your child lives in as well.

I long for heaven, because it is a place where troubles no longer exist and pain is a thing of the past. It's a place where everyone will be restored and Jimmy and I will experience the joy of meeting our daughter for the first time and get to know her like we've never known her before. What a great and wonderful day that will be.

HEAVENLY REST

I'm pooped. Are you too? I tend to blame my fatigue on having a child with special needs, but long before Dani was born I burned the candle at both ends. When I was a little girl, the first thing I'd say to my mother as she walked in the front door after work was, *"Are we going anywhere?"* I had to be annoying, but she was as patient as she could be with me.

In a day of fast-paced hustle bustle, it's difficult to find rest. The world turns at a pace that is faster than ever as we fill our calendars to the brim. We make and receive calls, respond to emails, send text messages, and work both inside and outside the home nearly every day of the year.

It's hard to find time to gather a thought, let alone take a moment of rest. Then there are all the concerns that go along with living in our modern world. *Where are the kids? Are they safe? Am I going to make it to the meeting on time with this horrible traffic? How are we going to have dinner when Johnny has two tournaments tonight? Where'd my purse go? All my money and ID is in that thing!*

Deadlines, safety, work, and schedules; they bombard us from every direction, leaving very little time for rest. It's enough to wear us ragged. Unless we purposely lock the door, turn off the phone, shut down the computer, and stop what we're doing, rest will be nothing but an interrupted dream that will never come true.

One of the most beautiful sights I have ever seen is Niagara Falls. With stunning beauty, crystal clear water cascades over the cliff at a speed and volume that'll blow your mind. It simply never ends as it flows on forever. It is absolutely gorgeous and when the sun is out, there is a continual rainbow to top it all off!

When Jimmy and I first arrived at Niagara, we soon realized we'd never see the falls up close unless we walked there on foot. Figuring we'd muddle our way to the site one way or another; our primary goal was to get rid of the car. Finding a recreational area close by, we grabbed the first parking spot we could find. Proud of our accomplishment and eagerly anticipating the view, we emerged from the car ready to go.

To my utter amazement, the first thing I heard all around us was the sound of roaring water. *"That's the sound of falls! We have to be very close. All we have to do is follow the sound."* I said, and that's precisely what we did. In no time at all we were standing before one of the most breathtaking sights God has given to this earth.

We walked the falls that day till our legs were ready to fall off. Going from one shop to another, we passed in and out of the cool mist of the water as we toured this majestic attraction. We shopped, ate, took pictures of every imaginable thing, and then proceeded to walk a little more. My feet were killing me.

At the end of the day, out of sheer exhaustion, we laid down in the shade on a park lawn. Manicured with meticulous care, every blade of grass was exactly the same height. Not a weed was in sight and not a hole or divot could be seen in the grass.

Nothing but a lush green velvety lawn for hundreds of yards all around, it was simply beautiful.

Flat on my back, I stared up into the equally pristine sky and couldn't believe what a perfect day it was. The temperature was about 70 degrees, the humidity was low, and there wasn't a bug to be found. It felt like paradise, and I was soaking up every minute of it.

As I savored these dear moments of bliss, I proceeded to do what I never do in public. Some people do it in malls, others freely do it in airports, and men are notorious for it, but I never allow myself to do it anywhere but in my own home. But that day at Niagara was different. Throwing caution to the wind, I broke my own rule and did the unthinkable...I closed my eyes!

Yep, that's right. Out in the open and in a public setting I let down my guard and closed my eyelids. For once I didn't feel compelled to keep one eye on my purse or scan the crowd for any shady characters. I wasn't monitoring my personal space to see if anyone was invading it, I simply collapsed on the green bed of grass and enjoyed a little piece of heaven.

With fatigue saturating every fiber of my being, this tiny pleasure was a luxury. In fact, it was the exhaustion that made it so special. I didn't feel compelled to lie down and close my eyes when we first arrived at the falls because I was fresh and ready to go. I didn't feel the urge to do it at mid-day either since I still had a little more steam left in me. It wasn't till after a long day's journey of walking up and down the falls that I savored these precious moments of paradise.

The older I get; the wearier I feel sometimes. I don't have the energy I used to have, my body hurts in ways it never hurt before, and my heart aches under the burden of living in such a sinful world for 47 years.

Just this past week our city has been inundated with the news of a missing 18-year-old girl. When all was said and done, her simple trip to the store resulted in her abduction and murder. She graduated from high school two weeks prior and now she is gone. The violence is unfathomable and the pain unimaginable. It isn't the first time this kind of thing has happened, and it won't be the last. My heart hurts for the family and I long for the day of Christ's return.

The good news is, however, when we get to heaven we will find peace and rest. No more security alarms, chemotherapy, coming in before it gets dark, funerals, watching for child predators, putting up fences, or activating Amber alerts. Sickness, disease, violence, murder, and strife will all become a thing of the past.

I won't need to watch my purse, and you won't have to monitor your personal space. No one will have to lock their doors or windows, bugs and humidity will be gone and we'll be able to close our eyes whenever we want to.

Sealed by the Holy Spirit, we will be safe and secure in the hand of God forever. No one will be able to snatch us away from His hand, and as a result, peace and rest will be ours for eternity!

HEAVENLY REWARDS

One of the biggest challenges I've faced as the parent of a disabled child was discovering my purpose. Why do I do what I do and what's the deeper purpose? Why am I called to care for a child who will never be a productive member of society and how, if at all, does it impact the world?

I've shared this struggle with many people over the years only to discover they don't understand. I invariably hear, "*Your purpose is to care for your precious child*", as if I didn't already know. Of course I am here to care for my child, but why? Why me? Why her? Why this disability? Knowing that my job is to care for her isn't enough for me. I have to know why.

Only God knows all the reasons why He's allowed Dani's disabilities into our lives. Though Jimmy and I understand a few reasons why, the vast majority remain hidden in the mind of God. He knows what He's doing and I trust Him fully, but that doesn't stop me from asking questions from time to time.

Just recently I found myself asking God why, after nineteen years, I am still cleaning up poopy pants. I know it's a part of my job, but I want to know the deeper reason. Surely it's more than simply keeping her clean, as important as that is.

Why I'm in my late forties and still cleaning dirty pants I don't fully understand, but I have come to one conclusion. Cleaning messy pants hones within me greater strength, perseverance, and dedication.

Yes, having my hands in the toilet actually serves to improve who I am, because when I have to do what I don't want to do over and over again, my faith is challenged at its core. Prompting me to ask soul-searching questions, God allows the trials of life to push me to the point where I must make pivotal decisions regarding my walk with Him.

Will I turn from God or cling to my faith and walk with Him where I do not want to go? Will I give up and act like a child when I don't get my way or determine to persevere through? Can I trust in the One who calls me His own or will I doubt His love and follow the enemy?

The decisions I make in each trial are vital. Challenging me to decide who I will become, each one forces me to choose a direction. Like the turn of a steering wheel, they guide me in a direction that either brings me closer to God or veers me far away from Him. If I am angry and resentful as I clean up a mess, I am drifting farther away from God, but when I set my hope on Him and humbly do as I'm called to do, I enter into His presence and am blessed.

When all is said and done, doing these things for Dani ultimately molds me into a person that is more like Christ. His disabled lamb receives the loving care she deserves, and I reap eternal rewards in heaven. It's a win-win situation.

God is always faithful to reward those who are dedicated to Him, and I believe He makes a special point to compensate those who remain steadfast when they do not understand His plan. Fair-weather fans of faith are not listed among those commended in Hebrews 11. In fact, if you look at the names listed in this chapter, not one of them knew why God was calling them to do what He called them to do.

Abraham was told to leave his home and move to a new land, but he wasn't told where to go. Testing his faith and trust in God, he had to first leave his home, and then wait for God to lead him to his new destination.

Then, there were the parents of Moses who knew beyond a shadow of a doubt they had a special child, but didn't have a clue how to spare him from the hands of the tyrant king. With great faith and dedication, they made the painful decision to give him up rather than allow him to be killed. Setting him adrift on the Nile's alligator infested waters, they chose to trust God even when they did not understand (Exodus 2:1-10).

The people listed in God's "Hall of Faith" (Hebrews 11) discovered something we all need to know, which is the perfect blend of faith and dedication. As regular, everyday blue-collar folks these Biblical characters had what it took to follow God when all seemed a mystery. Even a pagan prostitute, Rahab, stood tall in faith and pleased God so much she's listed as one of the Old Testament greats.

Imagine how lost, abandoned, unworthy, insignificant, and outnumbered they all must have felt. Persecuted and condemned, many lost their lives over their convictions, yet never lost their faith.

Perhaps you feel insignificant too. Much of the work you do is unseen by everyone around you, making you wonder why you do it at all. You've heard it said, out of sight is out of mind. Well, with humans this is true, but never with God. He sees everything we do, even if another soul on earth does not.

He sees the mother's hand in the middle of the night as it gently stokes the feverish brow of her little child. He grins as a little girl's daddy lifts her high atop his shoulders for the sole purpose of making her giggle, and He hears the quiet kiss of a mother as her lips gently touch the sticky cheek of her toddler.

Few witness these touching scenes, but God sees them all. Tallying the score like a referee on the sidelines, He takes note of everything we do, chalking it all up toward a heavenly reward.

As one who thrives on seeing the benefit of my labors, this bit of knowledge does me a world of good. Just writing this book has been a labor of love that's been in the works for over a year.

All this time, not one person has seen so much as a word, except for my son who's just begun proofreading.

Even Jimmy hasn't read a single word. He sees me slip out of bed in the wee hours of the morning, go down and sit at my computer, but hasn't actually seen what I've written.

I couldn't begin to count the hours it's taken to write this book, and I confess there have been mornings when I've sat down to write and thought to myself, *"What in the world am I doing? Will this help anyone? Could this be in vain? Does God really have a purpose and goal with this book?"*

But somehow, in spite of the questions and doubts, I continue to move toward the goal, trusting God has a plan and purpose.

I imagine Matthias had similar questions run through his mind a time or two as well. As one well known for not being known, I wouldn't be surprised if his name doesn't even ring a bell. It's quite possible you can't even pronounce his name, let alone describe who he was or what he did. If so, I rest my case. He is one of the Bible's most behind-the-scenes guys.

Present and active throughout Christ's entire ministry, Matthias is not mentioned until after the ascension in Acts 1. A faithful follower with the disciples, not a peep is heard of him until Jesus was killed, buried and rose again. Then suddenly, as if pulled from the back seat of a theater, he's brought onto the stage and given a vital role.

What prompted the mention of Matthias after standing in the wings for so long? Why was he suddenly put into action and brought to the forefront? Peter explained it all in a prayer meeting.

With Judas gone, the position of the twelfth disciple was vacant and needed be filled, according to Acts 1:20, Psalm 69:25, and Psalm 109:8. After a time of prayer about who could fill these important shoes, only two men met the qualifications. A man named Joseph and another named Matthias. Lots were cast, as was the custom of the day, and soon it was clear God had chosen Matthias.

Of all the men in the region, only two men fit the bill, and of the two, God chose Matthias. What an esteemed honor and compliment. Speaking of his impeccable faith, character, and devotion, becoming the twelfth disciple had to be a promotion to end all promotions!

Just think about how many people swarmed around Jesus and His disciples during His three-year ministry. Much of the time it was as if Jesus and His miracles was the newest craze in town, prompting many to follow Him. But when all was said and done, and a man had to be chosen, only two men fit the bill, and only one could be chosen.

Matthias didn't know it at the time, but he had been in a three-year job interview. As one who was observed closely day after day, his character was under intense scrutiny, until the time came for his final evaluation. With Judas dead and Jesus gone, the decision had to be made who would fill this position and Matthias was in the running.

To the naked eye, Matthias was just an average man, seemingly hidden as he worked behind the scenes. I wouldn't doubt if no one thought a thing of the guy prior to his nomination. He was just dependable Matt, the guy who was always there and never caused any trouble. No big deal.

But God had been watching him and hadn't forgotten a thing. Watching his every move, observing his faith, and noting his tenacious dedication, God was planning and calculating Matthias' reward. It was going to be very special, unique, and wonderfully unexpected.

Not much is known about Matthias and what he did here on earth. He simply did his work for the Lord and asked for nothing more. But God never allows our work for Him to go unrewarded. He is always keeping score in hopes to grant the greatest gift possible

While history may not speak much of Matthias and all the things he did here on earth, the Bible clearly reveals one of his heavenly rewards, which we will all see throughout eternity. Let's take a look at it and share in his excitement.

"The wall of the city had twelve foundations, and on them were the names of the twelve apostles of the Lamb."

(Revelation 21:14)

Just think about it. For eternity, the name Matthias will never be forgotten or missed, not even for a moment. Once quiet and unknown, the name Matthias is permanently written in the twelve foundations of the city of the New Jerusalem for all to see in eternity.

Everyone, no matter who we are or where we go, will see his name listed with the other eleven disciples. No one else in history sits among these twelve who were chosen to found God's New Testament church, but Matthias is now one of them.

Never mentioned as one of Jesus' inner circle, or one who ate with Him at the table, Matthias worked hard for God behind the scenes during Jesus' public ministry, yet was never overlooked. His love and devotion for Christ was real and true. He was a genuine follower who loved the Lord, and because of that, his name is written in heaven!

The last man picked for the team, the one who didn't give in and refused to give up, got to play in the last play of the Super Bowl, and now wears a ring to prove it. Doesn't that just warm your heart? Aren't you just thrilled on his behalf?

I've often wondered how Matthias felt during the years he followed Christ at such close but obscure range. Did he ever look at the disciples and wish he were in their shoes? Did he ever feel any angst over the fact he wasn't in the limelight, or was he content on the sidelines quietly serving God?

I'd like to think he felt a few feelings of jealousy a time or two, because if he did, I'd feel a lot better about myself. As one hidden in obscurity, I often wonder what it would be like to work for God out in the world. I love God with all my heart; I study His word and seek to apply it to my life every day, but I have to confess I still have a strong desire to work for Him out in the real world from time to time.

Perhaps you can relate to this struggle as well. Maybe life feels like a straightjacket that is holding you back from all you want to do. If this is how you feel, I understand, but caution you to be very careful. I know from experience the disasters discontent can bring. Like a tiny patch of ice it can send us sailing. And before we know it, we're flat on our back in a daze, wondering how we ever lost our footing.

Our first goal in life is to always be in the center of God's will, no matter where that may be. Whether we are on the sidelines cleaning up messes or in the middle of the Super Bowl game, God is the one we are to have our sights set on and nothing else.

Think for a moment what would have happened if Matthias had become dissatisfied and given up while Jesus was still alive. What if during Christ's ministry he stood up from obscurity and said, *"I give up! I'm just as good as the twelve you've chosen and if I can't do what they do, I'm not following You anymore. I am tired of being a nobody, so I'm gone."*

Imagine him packing his bags and leaving in a huff, determined to find greener pastures on his own. Think of the heavenly blessings he would have unwittingly forfeited, all for an earthly reward that would pass like a fleeting wind.

At the time, Matthias had no way of knowing the repercussions either decision might bring, but today we do. Looking back on his story it's clear to see that when we do what God calls us to do, and remain faithful to the task, unimaginable blessings are guaranteed!

I love the story of Matthias. I can relate to his obscurity, and I admire his dedication. Building a pristine resume while simply doing what God had called him to do, he earned a reward only twelve men in history now possess.

Do you wonder why God has you where you are and what your purpose in life is? Does the thought of caring for a disabled child the rest of your life bring feelings of dread and fear? I suspect the enemy is hard at work to make you feel insignificant, worthless, and invisible. He has you discouraged and doubtful of the future, and perhaps has you blaming it all on your child's disability.

If this is the case, let me encourage you to put your trust in God. He is extremely creative and always in the midst of doing fantastic things we can't begin to comprehend.

Consider for a moment, the fact that God has chosen you for just such a time as this. It is no mistake you are the parent of your child, and it's no oversight your child is the way he or she is. God sees and knows everything. Nothing slips past His wisdom, and no child of His is indigent or poor. Everything that has come into your life has been strategically allowed according to His sovereign will and design. He knows precisely where you are, what you need, and how to best provide for you.

You *can* handle the situation you are in. You don't have to settle for simply surviving. Your life can bloom and thrive in spite of any disability, but you must place God first in your life today. Once you have done this, you and your family will be blessed beyond measure.

How I pray you find the will of God for your life. It's simply too good to miss. It is custom built just for you and much more than you would ever expect. Determine to persevere through your tribulations and never lose hope. Keep your eyes on God and trust Him with your future, then you'll be amazed at what God will do!

EPILOGUE

By the time Dani was three years old, she was clearly bound by Autism. Never crying for my husband or me, and refusing to be held, she was virtually walled off from the world around her. Each passing day broke our hearts as we watched the chasm grow wider and wider.

In desperation one day, we made the decision to attempt to bring her into our world. We were driving down the highway discussing how to accomplish this when I felt compelled to say, *"But what gives us the right to bring her into our world? With so much pain and suffering do we really want to bring her into it? Maybe she would be best left in her own world."*

With wisdom my husband replied, *"There are a lot of good things in our world, too. You and I are two good things in this world she is missing and we have a lot to offer her. She needs to meet her parents."* I couldn't dispute the logic, so we commenced with a plan.

God gave us the idea to do a therapy, something I'd never heard of before. On the premise that every human needs physical contact, we decided to begin holding Dani, even though she would most certainly not like it a bit.

Talk about tough love, this was downright painful for everyone. But there was no doubt about it, she needed as much human contact as we could give her in order for her to improve.

So, each day I began doing what we call "hold therapy." I would wrap her arms and legs around my body and hold her firmly as she would begin to scream. With her head on my chest I would rock her gently and stroke her back as I gently whispered to her that everything was all right. She was still relatively small so I could keep her in my arms, but she fought and screamed as if I were sticking pins in her.

The plan was to hold her until she was too physically exhausted to cry. After that, the goal was for her to collapse in my arms and feel my loving embrace for the first time. Even if we connected for just a few seconds, Jimmy and I felt this could be a way to introduce ourselves to our little girl. Maybe then she would want to join us in our world.

The first session, she screamed forty minutes straight until she finally collapsed. I comforted her as long as she would allow, then let her down and waited to do it again the next day.

After a week and a half, the time spent crying began to shorten. Over time we gained the ability to hold her without a fight at all, and today she not only acknowledges us as her parents, but also enjoys a good hug and cuddle on the couch like any other child.

Sometimes children of God need a little hold therapy too. Like those afflicted with Autism, God seeks to hold us, but we pull away and retreat into our own little world. We need Him more than anything else, yet we kick, scream, and fuss to get away.

The more I live and deal with Dani's disabilities, the more I see how disabled I am as well. I am far too independent, self-reliant, selfish, prideful, fearful, and controlling. I have to be told repeatedly to do something, and when I finally do it, I invariably try to put my own spin on it. I am slow to respond and eager to run away. I bite the hand that feeds me, and then wonder why I'm hungry, yet God loves me through it all.

Why does God love me? The same reason He loves you. He is our Creator and we are His prized possessions. He wants us to be free, so He sent His Son Jesus to die on the cross for our sins.

If by chance you do not know Him today, turn a few pages and pray a simple prayer. God is waiting for you, and His Son Jesus is ready to show you the way. The enemy doesn't want you to discover intimacy with God, because He doesn't want you to be free. He wants you miserable, unhappy, and useless, but that is not the destiny God has for you.

Learn to distinguish between the lies of the enemy and the truth of God, and then follow God's truth to liberty. It is a gift from God and yours for the taking, so take it today and discover the true freedom God has waiting for you!

NANCY AND DANI

"I will walk about in freedom,

for I have sought out your precepts."

Psalm 119:45

Are You Ready for Eternity?

If you were to die today, do you know where you would go? Would you spend eternity in heaven with God, or be subject to perpetual hell?

In our busy world it is easy not to think about this question. We often only live in the here and now. But, we all have an appointed time in which we will die, and each day brings this moment closer.

Where will you go? Where will your family members go? All of us are sinners and in need of a Savior (Romans 3:23). You need a Savior, and I need one too. God's Word tells us the *only* way we can enter into heaven is through His Son Jesus Christ (Romans 6:23). Our sin creates a debt none of us will ever be able to pay. He paid the debt once and for all; we need only believe.

Do you believe in Jesus? Do you believe He is God's Son and the only way into heaven? Please don't mistake believing in Jesus as simply knowing of Him. Even Satan knows of Jesus. They've met on numerous occasions.

Knowing *of* Jesus and believing *in* Him are two different things. To believe means to put your faith and trust in Him, to follow Him in all your ways, and obey His commands. It is to read His Word and allow it to sink into your heart so that you can become more like Him. It involves loving Him more than you love yourself and offering your life as a living sacrifice to Him and His Father's will.

I firmly believe that if you cannot name a specific date in which you accepted Christ, there is a good chance you are not saved. Why take the chance? Accept Jesus as your Savior today. Invite Him into your heart, and write this date in a special place, such as in this book or the front of your Bible.

Salvation is permanent and eternal (John 10:27, Ephesians 4:30, 2 Corinthians 1:22). It can never be taken away from you. God is faithful to hear your prayer and seal you as one of His own right now. All you need is to sincerely pray a prayer similar to this:

Dear Jesus,

I know I am a sinner. I believe you died on the cross and paid the penalty for my sins. I believe you rose from the dead after three days in the grave and I repent from my sins. I place my faith and trust in you and you alone. Thank you for giving me eternal life!

In Jesus' name, Amen.

_____(Your name)

_____(Today's date)

Congratulations! You are now a child of God.

I'd Love to Hear from You!

Thank you for joining me in the pages of Freedom. I pray the Lord has enlightened you in a fresh new way. My hope is that through my story, you too have found greater healing, strength, and true freedom.

There is no doubt in my mind God has a unique and special plan for you as the parent of a child with special needs, one that only you can fulfill. If you would like to let me know how God has spoken to your heart, contact me at:
www.oliveleafministries.com

In Christ,

Nancy Douglas

Also Available from Nancy Douglas

Draw Me Near

Pursuing an Intimate Relationship with God

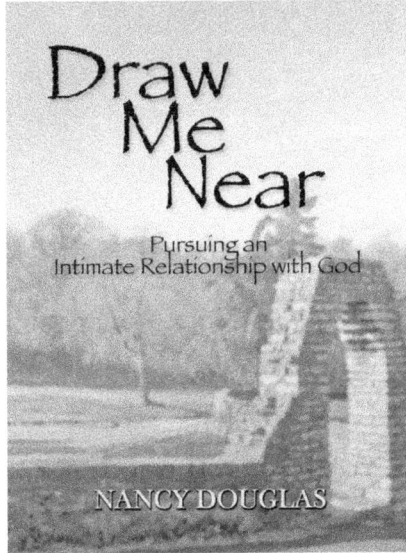

How is your level of intimacy with God? Is it all you want it to be? Better yet, is it all God wants it to be? Throughout history, man has struggled to achieve closeness with the heart of God. But there is more to intimacy with God than simply knowing who He is. The real secret lies within ourselves and our willingness to be honest with Him. Honesty is truly the best policy. This is particularly true when seeking God.

This 10-week study is specifically designed to deepen your walk with God. Whether a seasoned Christian or brand new, it will help you draw closer to Him. The journey is challenging, fun, and enlightening as it takes you to places you've never been before. You'll begin your study on one shore only to find yourself on another as you embark on your new voyage with God.

Coming Fall 2008

ONE SIZE FITS ALL

A WOMAN'S ATTIRE FOR SPIRITUAL SUCCESS

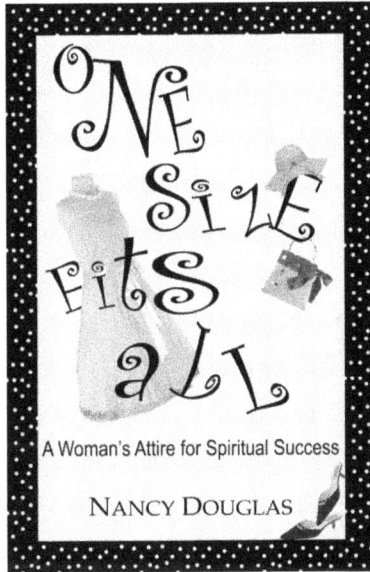

Are you dressed for spiritual success? In One Size Fits All, discover how to prepare yourself each day by putting on the armor of God. Geared specifically for women and their unique needs, this book is fun, enlightening and sure to change your life. Look for it coming soon in a bookstore near you or visit: oliveleafministries.com

www.ingramcontent.com/pod-product-compliance
Lightning Source LLC
Chambersburg PA
CBHW031836090426

42741CB00005B/259